CLOSE READING NEW MEDIA

Symbolae

Facultatis Litterarum Lovaniensis

SERIES D LITTERARIA
VOL. 16

SYMBOLAE, series D LITTERARIA, a collection of studies edited by
the department of Literary Studies of The Faculty of Arts
at the 'Katholieke Universiteit Leuven' (Louvain, Belgium).

CLOSE READING NEW MEDIA

Analyzing Electronic Literature

edited by
Jan VAN LOOY
and
Jan BAETENS

Leuven University Press
2003

Published with the support of
K.U.Leuven Commissie voor Publicaties

© 2003 Universitaire Pers Leuven / Presses Universitaires de Louvain / Leuven University Press
Blijde-Inkomststraat 5, B-3000 Leuven (Belgium)

All rights reserved. Except in those cases expressly determined by law, no part of this publication may be multiplied, saved in an automated datafile or made public in any way whatsoever without the express prior written consent of the publishers.

ISBN 90 5867 323 5
D / 2003 / 1869 / 48
NUR: 635

Cover photo: Bruno Vandermeulen, Jan Van Looy
Cover design: Lejan Tits

Contents

Introduction: Close Reading Electronic Literature 7
    Jan Van Looy & Jan Baetens (K.U.Leuven)

I. Hypertext

Stephanie Strickland's *True North*: A Migration between Media . . 27
    Joseph Tabbi (University of Illinois – Chicago)
Sutured Fragments: Shelley Jackson's *Patchwork Girl* in Piecework . 39
    Elisabeth Joyce (Edinboro University of Pennsylvania)
In Search of *Califia* 53
    Raine Koskimaa (IT University of Copenhagen)

II. Internet Text

Underground Lies: Revisiting Narrative in Hyperfiction . . . .
    Richard Saint-Gelais & René Audet (CRELIQ/Université Laval)
Stealing or giving? On Raymond Federman's & Anne Burdick's
Eating Books 71
    Jan Baetens (K.U.Leuven)
One must be Calm and Laugh: Geoff Ryman's Web Novel *253* as a
Hypertextual Contemplation on Modernity 87
    Jan Van Looy (K.U.Leuven)

III. Cybertext

Requiem for a Reader? A Semiotic Approach to Reader and Text in
Electronic Literature 123
    Jack Post (University of Maastricht)

The Narrative of an Interface: Rethinking Hypertext Theory by Facing Design Questions 141
  Paul A. Harris (Loyola Marymount University)
Hypertextual Consciousness: Notes toward a Critical Net Practice . 157
  Mark Amerika (University of Colorado – Boulder)

About the Contributors 177

Appendix: Electronic Literature on the Web 181

Introduction:
Close Reading Electronic Literature

Jan Van Looy & Jan Baetens
(K.U.Leuven)

Since the early 1990s electronic art and literature have continually gained importance both in artistic and in academic circles. Significant critical and theoretical attention has been paid to how new media allows the text to break with traditional power relations and boundaries. The passive reader becomes an active participant choosing his own path and assembling not just his own interpretation of the text (level of the signified), but also his own text (level of the signifier). Texts no longer have a beginning or an ending being a web of interlinked nodes or rhizome (Deleuze & Guattari through Landow 1997: 38). The decentered nature of electronic text empowers and invites the reader to take part in the literary process. Poststructuralist theorists predicted a total liberation of textual restrictions imposed by the medium of print. However, while these are culturally significant claims, little attention has been paid to their realization, with the notable exception of Silvio Gaggi, who, in the last chapter of *From text to hypertext,* provides a thorough analysis of two landmarks of hyperfiction: Michael Joyce's *Afternoon* (1990) and Stuart Moulthrop's *Victory Garden* (1991). The goal of this volume is twofold. First, our aim is to shed some light on how ideas and theories have been translated into concrete works. Second, we want to comment on the process of close reading and how it can be applied to electronic literature. Although all contributions deal with particular works, their aim is always to provide insight into how electronic fiction and poetry are read.

To our knowledge this is the first publication to explicitly apply the method of 'close reading' to electronic literature. Why this is the case is not too difficult to explain. When surveying the reasons why the minute and patient reading of concrete texts has not yet seduced contemporary scholars, we can list a number of explanations which largely reinforce each other. First of all there is the basic conviction that critical attention does not matter, or even that it is not appropriate to works belonging to a medium which has as one of its primary principles the absence of – literally – fixed shapes and – literally – fixed meanings (cf. Manovich 2001: 36). We must add 'literally', since we should not forget that in the traditional view, close reading does not aim to produce *the* meaning of *the* text, but rather to unearth all possible types of ambiguities and irony. Second, there is the idea, which is not entirely false, that hyperfiction is born on the margins of a medium, the computer, which is still considered a number cruncher rather than a literary device. Like in the first years of cinema, when films were made to promote the marketing of projection and recording machines, the important thing is not the message but the apparatus. With Aarseth we do not agree with this standpoint. "The emerging new media technologies are not important in themselves, nor as alternatives to older media, but should be studied for what they can tell us about the principles and evolution of human communication" (Aarseth 1997: 17). Third, we often hear the argument that hyperfiction has not yet produced enough interesting works to justify a turn towards a more literal and literary tackling of the material. We would like to contend this view by pointing at the fact that even if there is not yet any 'high literature' in the electronic realm, its works can still be significant. "For the literary scholar, the importance of the electronic movement is twofold: it problematizes familiar notions, and it challenges the limits of language" (Ryan 1999: 10).

From a more theoretical standpoint, we would like to defend the cause of close reading scholarship by referring to two authors whose insights shed new light on the problem of close reading: Jacques Fontanille, currently the leading French semiotician, and Stanley Cavell. In the preface to *Littérature, Informatique, Lecture*, a publication on hypertext and electronic literature, Jacques Fontanille argues that there is a world of difference between on the one hand the text as an *object* (as a set of material elements and instructions) and on the other hand the text as a *discursive* unit (as a more or less coherent set of interpretations the reader produces in order to make sense of it). Fontanille claims that the only way to read hyperfiction thoroughly is to read it as we have learnt to read texts: slowly, with much effort, continually going forward and backward, not by clicking, navigating or experiencing randomly. The only way to act as a *free* reader is not to read more rapidly, but, on the contrary, to slow down, to look into details, to build up a framework brick after brick. We need to be able to establish a dialogue with the forms, the structures, and the meanings of both the text and the hypertext. Until that has happened, a (hyper)text cannot become a discourse, i.e. a meaningful whole grasped by a conscious reader (Fontanille 1999).

In *The World Viewed* (1979) the philosopher Stanley Cavell develops a media theory containing a superb plea for close reading of media in general and film in particular. His examples of close reading, collected in *Pursuits of Happiness* (1981), should convince even the harshest enemy that the time one takes to read an image is never lost. Given the fact that cinema is a medium of which the 'essence' is difficult to define both chronologically (today's cinema is very different from what is now being called 'the early cinema') and syntagmatically (it has never been easy to mark clear-cut frontiers between film and other visual media), Cavell has been challenged to elaborate a theoretical framework, which is able to take into account the fundamental dialectics between closure and openness of a medium. Media exist, of course, but the way we consider and use them shifts through time and space. In order to solve this problem (insoluble from an essentialist or technologist perspective), Cavell proposes a definition of media which relies on a threefold thesis. (1) A medium cannot be discussed without its concrete 'output'; no media theory can be established without the analysis of concrete works. (2) A medium does not exist before concrete works embody it, otherwise its existence is merely virtual, since nobody recognizes it as an independent medium. (3) Those concrete works, and hence the media they forge, only exist when forms become 'meaningful', i.e. are considered not simply a formal device, but also an element which models a certain signification in a certain medium. The close-up, for example, was a form of amusement in early cinema until it became motivated in narrative cinema. Finally, Cavell argues that the 'birth' of a medium always depends on the creation of an 'automatism', while the creation of an automatism also implies the transformation of a medium. Hence the definition Cavell provides for the concept of medium is very close to that of genre, which is all but illogical from his viewpoint.

There are numerous meanings to the verb 'to read' and its origins are rather obscure, as the *Oxford English Dictionary* informs us. Earliest Teutonic and Sanscrit precursors designate acts of 'deliberation', 'consideration', 'giving thought or attendance to' or refer to 'success' or 'accomplishment'. Later definitions complicate matters even further. A rather obscure meaning of 'read' is its use as a noun signifying 'stomach of an animal'. This sense is possibly the oldest of meanings and uses. Hence it is possible that all other meanings have developed from the practice to prognosticate, discern, or otherwise interpret good and bad fortune, by perusing the innards of animals. (Wolfreys 2000: ix). Reading is always an act of dismemberment, of tearing open in search of hidden meanings. 'Close' as in 'close reading' has come to mean 'in an attentive manner', but in the expression 'to pay close attention', for example, we still have a sense of nearness. When close reading, the eyes of the reader are almost touching the words of the text. Nothing is to escape the attention of the meticulous scholar. Every small discontinuity, contradiction or aporia is identified and written down for further reference. While the meaning of 'close' can imply 'near in relationship' as in 'close relative' or 'intimate or confidential' as in 'close friends', when it comes to 'close reading' there is a sense of hostility between the reader and the text. The text is never trusted at face value, but is torn to pieces and reconstituted by a reader who is always at the same time a demolisher and a constructor.

In the 1980s and 90s proponents of hypertext literature like George Landow, Michael Joyce, Stuart Moulthrop and Jay David Bolter presented hyperfiction as the fulfillment of poststructuralist literary theory. Links were considered the materialization of intertextuality. Bricolage or tinkering (Turkle 1995) was hailed as a liberation of the act of writing and hypertext was described by concepts like decentering, writerly reader (Barthes 1974 through Landow 1997) and différance (Derrida 1967). Conversely, adversaries of the hyperfiction aesthetic (e.g. Birkerts 1994) swore by the warm comforting authorial voice of the novel and associated hyperfiction with being lost in an infinite maze trying to extract meaning out of the meaningless. We will not pursue this discussion any further here. For our purposes, it suffices to note that the dispute revolves around the opposition between 'looking at' and 'looking into', between being confronted with and being submerged in the text.

In *Remediation* (1999), Bolter and Grusin analyze media history teleologically through the opposition between *hypermediacy* and *immediacy*. Both tendencies are described as manifestations of a mimetic desire, a desire to depict reality. Through hypermediacy culture attempts to attain more direct representation by multiplying media, by saturating itself with sources of information. As the name suggests, hypermediacy is associated with hypertext and it may well have been inspired by the typical news Web site at the end of the nineties where text is combined with images, animation and film. Hypermediatic design is described as privileging "fragmentation, indeterminacy, and heterogeneity and... emphasiz[ing] process or performance rather than the finished art object" (31). Hypermediacy urges the user not only to look at the interface, but also to actively participate in the communication and meaning generation process by offering multiple channels and paths which he may choose to engage in. Through the logic of transparent immediacy, on the other hand, culture strives "to erase or to render automatic the act of representation"(33). The medium attempts to efface itself so as to present the mediated world as a unified visual space, seamlessly integrated in the environment. The most prototypical example here is probably the Cinema Theater where the viewer is submerged in images, sound and darkness.

In *Narrative as Virtual Reality* (2001), Marie-Laure Ryan starts from the definition of virtual reality by Pimentel and Teixeira as an "interactive immersive experience generated by a computer" (2). From this definition she derives two dimensions – immersion and interactivity – which she develops into the "cornerstones of a phenomenology of reading, or, more broadly, of art experiencing" (2). She does this by situating the two concepts in the history of western art which "has seen the rise and fall of immersive ideals, and their displacement, in the twentieth century, by an aesthetics of play and self-reflexivity that eventually produced the ideal of an active participation of the appreciator – reader, spectator, user – in the production of the text" (2). Importantly, like Bolter and Grusin, she describes immersion and interactivity as opposed forces, which she sees as interacting and leading to an ultimate goal in the history of representation, the sublimation of the two concepts in virtual reality. Thereby, she associates the aesthetics of immersion with a "'world' that serves as environment for a virtual body," and that of interactivity as a text presented as a "game, language as a plaything, and the reader as the player" (16), descriptions that clearly derive from poststructuralist theory as it was advanced by hypertext theorists.

In the fourth chapter of *The Language of New Media* (2001) titled "The illusions" Lev Manovich invokes a similar opposition. "In the twentieth century, art has largely rejected the goal of illusionism, the goal that was so important to it before; as a consequence, it has lost much of its popular support. The production of illusionistic representations has become the domain of mass culture and of media technologies – photography, film, and video" (177). But Manovich does not directly associate the artistic side of the opposition with interactivity. Instead, in the fifth subsection called "Illusion, Narrative, and Interactivity," he confronts illusion (cf. looking through, immediacy, immersion) with interaction as two concepts from a different realm that work with and against each other. More precisely, he notes that many digital artifacts "are characterized by a peculiar temporal dynamic – a constant, repetitive oscillation between an illusion and its suspense. These new media objects keep reminding us of their artificiality, incompleteness, and constructedness. They present us with a perfect illusion only next to reveal its underlying machinery" (205).

While there seems to be a consensus amongst contemporary theorists on the fact that experiencing new media is strongly tied to the opposition between 'in' and 'at', between 'immediacy' and 'hypermediacy', between 'immersion' and 'interactivity', this temporal dynamics far from explains everything (see also Van Looy forthcoming). New media theory needs a solid description of how interactivity influences meaning generation in order to be able to tackle socially significant issues like violence in videogames and Internet regulation. This volume by no means provides this theory, but it does attempt to give a genuine account of the workings of nine electronic texts in order to point to, rather than theorize, interesting points and problematics. In the next paragraph we have gathered some of the questions that are raised.

What does it mean to read electronic text? How do we deal with changeability and multilinearity? Can we read multimedia content? And what is its status in the reading? Does it contribute to the meaning of the text or is it merely surface? Is it only a catalyst, some sweets to keep the attention of the reader, or does it introduce a new kind of writing where the monopoly of the alphabetic sign is definitively broken? What happens if there is no longer one central text? Citation, 'collage' and sampling pull the exterior into the interior. Linking to illustrative material, secondary literature turn the interior inside out and show that a text is never an isolated act of wording. What does it mean to structure a text not only on the level of the signified, but also on the level of the signifier? How does the author apply these newly acquired skills to create new types of narrative? How does the narrative plane influence the hypertextual structuring and vice versa? How does a story emerge from a decentered body of hyperlinked, textual, pictorial, and multimedial materials? Can we still speak of one work or one narrative when its appearance is different in every reading? How does one grasp and control the proliferating number of texts and interpretations of texts? Is there such a thing as a hypertext, one text above all, one text including all others and what does this tell us about the act of writing and the functioning of culture? What happens when the inside of a work is indistinguishable from the outside, when linking undermines all sense of boundaries and direction? Does the reader become an author or, conversely, do the new literary devices give the author more opportunity to control meaning and to manipulate the reader into a certain configuration. Has the reader become a Writer? A Wreader?

Hypertext

In 1945, the same year that Eckert and Mauchly complete the first working electronic digital computer, the ENIAC, Vannevar Bush introduces his MEMEX (memory extender) project. In his Essay "As We May Think," Bush tries to find a solution to the growing problem of the inaccessibility of our archives.

> The difficulty seems to be, not so much that we publish unduly in view of the extent and variety of present day interests, but rather that publication has been extended far beyond our present ability to make real use of the record. The summation of human experience is being expanded at a prodigious rate, and the means we use for threading through the consequent maze to the momentarily important item is the same as was used in the days of square-rigged ships (Bush 1945).

Bush's interest is primarily encyclopedic; he wants to facilitate access to the record. While at one point in his essay he states "The advanced arithmetical machines of the future will be electrical in nature, and they will perform 100 times present speeds, or more," he still sees his MEMEX as a mechanical device based on microfilm and levers. "On deflecting one of these levers to the right [the user] runs through the book before him, each page in turn being projected at a speed which just allows a recognizing glance at each. If he deflects it further to the right, he steps through the book 10 pages at a time; still further at 100 pages at a time" (Bush 1945). More important than the technological details, however, is the fact that Bush proposes associative indexing as a new means to retrieve information and is therefore considered the inventor of the concept of hypertext.

> When the user is building a trail, he names it, inserts the name in his code book, and taps it out on his keyboard. Before him are the two items to be joined, projected onto adjacent viewing positions (...). The user taps a single key, and the items are permanently joined (...). Thereafter, at any time, when one of these items is in view, the other can be instantly recalled merely by tapping a button below the corresponding code space (Bush 1945).

In 1965 Theodor Holm (Ted) Nelson wrote the paper "A File Structure for the Complex, the Changing, and the Indeterminate" for the Association for Computing Machinery in which he coined the term 'hypertext'. Hypertext is a conjunction of 'text' and the Old Greek 'ὑπερ' (hyper) meaning 'over, above, beyond, besides'. In *Literary Machines* (1987) Nelson defines hypertext as "non-sequential writing – text that branches and allows choices to the reader, best read at an interactive screen." Examples of non-electronic hypertext like Cortazar's *Hopscotch* (1966) – the so-called proto-hypertexts – were attested years later when critics started seeing the resemblance between Nelson's ideas and developments in earlier experimental novel writing. Although Nelson repeatedly refers to Vannevar Bush – he even includes "As We May Think" as a chapter in *Literary Machines* – they have different conceptions of hypertext. Whereas Bush sees his MEMEX as a way to manipulate and search large amounts of stored knowledge, Nelson dreams of the ultimate centralized literary archive, which he named *Xanadu* after the imaginary utopia in Coleridge's "Kubla Khan." Unfortunately the system was never operational.

The Xanadu software remained as mythic as the place after which it was named. In *Dream Machines*, published in 1974, Nelson announced that it would be ready for release by 1976 (56). In the 1987 edition of *Literary Machines*, the due date was 1988 (0/5).

The development of Xanadu was given a large boost in early 1988 when Autodesk (the company which made their fortune from AutoCAD) bought the Xanadu Operating Company. Code for a prototype of part of the system was made public later that year. In an article published in *Byte* in January 1988, Nelson expected to be fully completed by 1991 (299). Then, nothing. Autodesk has since relinquished interest in Xanadu (Keep 1995).

In 1999 the source code for *Xanadu* was released and some programmers have said that, indeed, it resembled poetry rather than programming.

However, via numerous other systems – e.g. Apple's *Hypercard*, Eastgate's *Storyspace*, Tim Berners Lee's *World Wide Web* – hypertext has become the prototypical form of interactive textuality (while by no means the most interactive). In hypertext the reader determines the unfolding of the text by clicking or selecting certain areas on the screen called hyperlinks, after which the screen reloads and presents another part of the text (node, lexia, page). Every segment can contain more than one hyperlink and if this is the case, each path taken by the reader can produce a different text (if we take text to be a sequence of signs). "Whereas the reader of a standard print text constructs personalized interpretation out of an invariant semiotic base, the reader of an interactive text thus participates in the construction of the text as a visible display of signs" (Ryan 2001: 5). The question whether each reading should be considered a different text or rather one view of the whole (somewhat like one chapter in a book) is taken up by Koskimaa further in this volume.

The analogy between postmodern aesthetics or poststructuralist thinking and the idea of interactivity and hypertext have been systematically developed by the early theorists of hypertext, such as George Landow, Jay David Bolter, Michael Joyce, and Stuart Moulthrop. As Marie-Laure Ryan notes in *Narrative as Virtual Reality: Immersion and Interactivity in Literature and Electronic Media* (2001), the list of features of hypertext that supports the postmodernist approach is impressive. "It is headed by Roland Barthes and Julia Kristeva's notion of 'intertextuality', the practice of integrating a variety of foreign discourses within a text through such mechanisms as quotation, commentary, parody, allusion, imitation, ironic transformation, rewrites, and decontextualizing / recontextualizing operations" (6). (This was also one of the principles Nelson had in mind when he invented hypertext, i.e. the materialization of literary connections, cf. *Literary Machines* [1987].) Moreover, hypertext supports what has been described by Lévi-Strauss as 'bricolage' or 'tinkering' as Sherry

Turkle calls it in *Life on the Screen* (1995). Finally, while linking can create connections between heterogeneous materials, it can also break apart elements thought to belong together. "The dismantling effect of hypertext is one more way to pursue the typically postmodern challenge of the epistemologically suspect coherence, rationality, and closure of narrative structures, one more way to deny the reader the satisfaction of a totalizing interpretation" (Ryan 2001: 7).

In the first essay of the hypertext-section, *Joseph Tabbi* analyzes the migration from print to electronic text of Stephanie Strickland's poem *True North* in an attempt to identify the forces that are transforming literary culture and its study in our time. In a prudent and thorough manner he describes how hypertext as method of annotation can bring about subtle shifts of meaning. Examples of references used to create a context of reading and interpretation are Emily Dickinson's poetry and Muriel Rukeyser's 1942 biography of Josiah Gibbs. As Tabbi shows, the introduction of the new in poetry requires a re-adjustment of all the mental categories by which we have come to know and recognize poetry. Strickland's poetics of indirect citation, annotation, and recombination creates affinities with a distinctive tradition that reaches back to Jonathan Edwards. Her willingness to court abstraction and a minimalist language opens what should be a fruitful conversation with the Language Poets, while the recognition awarded *True North* by the judges for the Sandeen Prize ensures that her work will be seen as contemporary social realism. Tabbi welcomes Strickland's engagement with the new medium which is endlessly more refreshing than those anthology CD-ROMs, published by Norton and others only because they could not make the paper any thinner. "Strickland's achievement is to locate the poetic possibilities inherent in the new medium, such that imagination might find expression in tags and numbers and nested programs no less than in words."

In "Sutured Fragments" *Elizabeth Joyce* describes how Shelley Jackson's *Patchwork Girl* uses the map as a metaphor for the body and as an analogy of the impress of cultural structures on geographical space as well as on the subjectivity of the individual. The identity of a girl is depicted through the grid of the map on three levels: hypertextual, narratological and corporeal which is closely related to the theme of hypertext reading as movement. The incorporation of texts from Mary Shelley's *Frankenstein*, but also from Frank Oz's *The Patchwork Girl of Oz*, Barbara Maria Stafford's *Body Criticism: Imaging the Unseen in Enlightenment Art and Medicine*, and others serves to snap the threads of the linear progression of a plot, rupturing repeatedly the reader's efforts to piece together the story. Just as Dr. Frankenstein sews together the monster's body from body parts gleaned from corpses, the girl's body is an appropriation of human remains, each fragment still imbued with the character of its original owner. Like hypertext, identity is never fixed or isolated, it is a cultural construction built up from discourses we appropriate at different occasions. This is what *Patchwork Girl* endeavors to do, to create the girl's body and by extension her identity by piecing together textual components that at the same time create the physical but also the conceptual entity of the text itself. The text enables, as in Deleuze and Guattari's model of subjectivity, the representation of the focus of manifold threads of meaning that bind together to form individual identity. According to Joyce, it is not merely a poststructuralist statement, however, but also an attempt to grasp human existence as heterogeneous in nature, as reflective of individual experiences and components that assemble within one body, all the parts of which continue to yell about their other contexts, their other states of being in the same way that the patchwork girl's physical parts retain allegiances to their first owner.

In the third and last essay of the hypertext section *Raine Koskimaa* analyzes M. D. Coverley (Marjorie Luesebrink)'s *Califia* primarily in terms of time and space. He wonders why temporal issues have received so little critical attention in hypertext theory. He employs Luesebrink's own concepts of 'interface time' and 'cognitive time' to describe the oscillation between the virtual time in the narrative universe and the time spent manipulating the text. These temporal issues have thematic repercussions since in *Califia* real and historical time are clearly separated, whereas mythical time is constantly present. Real time is open, in a constant process of becoming, historical time is linear, and mythic time is cyclical. In *Califia* this is closely related to cyclical phenomena in nature, especially to celestial movements. Geographical maps are often juxtaposed with star charts and treasure maps. In this way, the fictional world is represented as a kind of proto-virtual reality, which depicts the hypertextual structure and sub-structures in a natural way. The juxtaposing of different or even incompatible spaces produces a *heterotopic space*. Space and time thematize the reading process itself to become an eternal circle of interpretation. Each new piece of information is first, provisionally, interpreted from the viewpoint of the whole, but also carries with it the potential to change the larger picture and previous interpretations.

Internet Text

Today, the Internet has become a synonym of World Wide Web. However, when we look at the history of the Internet, the WWW is a relatively recent development. In 1969 Arpanet, an ancestor of the Internet, was commissioned to serve for research into networking between different universities. *File transfer* was the most important if not the only utilization of the network in those days. In the 1970s *email* was introduced, and by 1973 it accounted for 75% of byte traffic on Arpanet. In 1974 *telnet*, a protocol allowing to operate a system remotely was implemented, and around 1979 the first *Usenet* newsgroups appeared. Also in 1979, two students from Essex University, Richard Bartle and Roy Trubshaw, built the first *multi-user dungeon* (MUD), an online interactive text-based combat game. Finally, in 1988 Jarkko Oikarinen developed *Internet Relay Chat*, which for the first time allowed for large-scale real-time communication over the Net.

At that moment the need for a device for accessing structured information via the Internet was growing. In 1991, *Wide Area Information Servers* (WAIS) was invented by Brewster Kahle. WAIS is a system that allows indexing and accessing information from distributed databases. The user enters a search argument and the client program accesses all necessary servers. The results provide a description of each text that meets the search requirements. The user can then retrieve the full text. Also in 1991 Paul Lindner and Mark P. McCahill released *Gopher*, an Internet application protocol which permits hierarchically organized file systems to be maintained on servers which are part of an overall information structure. Importantly, Gopher provides a way to bring text files from all over the world to a viewer on your computer, just like a browser does for the World Wide Web today. However, neither Gopher nor WAIS is hypertextual in any way. Links between related nodes cannot be established freely; they are restricted by the organization of the overall database structure, which may be powerful, yet too rigid for some purposes.

In May 1991, the *World Wide Web* was officially released by CERN in Switzerland. Whereas Gopher and WAIS were conceived from an engineering aesthetic, the World Wide Web was a literary invention. Tim Berners-Lee – who developed http (HyperText Transfer Protocol), html (HyperText Markup Language) and who is the driving force behind the World Wide Web and the W3C consortium – points to Doug Engelbart's *oNLine System* (NLS), Vannevar Bush's "As We May Think" (1945) and Ted Nelson's *Literary Machines* (1987) as his major influences. Like Gopher, the World Wide Web allows the user to access information from anywhere in the world and display it directly in a client viewer (browser). However, thanks to its hypertextual organization, WWW is not restricted to a strictly hierarchical database structure. Instead, nodes can be freely interlinked, and decentered networks can be built based on associative structuring. "The whole point about hypertext was that (unlike most project management and documentation systems) [database systems, eds.] it could model a changing morass of relationships which characterized most real environments I knew (and certainly CERN)" (Berners-Lee 2000).

When WWW appeared, ftp (file transfer protocol) and Telnet were the most popular Internet services and Gopher was becoming increasingly popular. However, the user-friendliness and openness of its hypertext system caused WWW to quickly gain terrain. By March 1994 WWW byte-traffic passes Gopher byte-traffic on NSFnet. Moreover, later that year WWW edges out Telnet to become the second most popular service on the Net (behind ftp). The true boom with the consequent democratization of the Internet appears when James Clark and Marc Andreessen release *NCSA Mosaic*, the browser that will later become *Netscape Navigator*. With Mosaic the first graphics appear on the Web.

In the first essay of the Internet text section, *Richard Saint-Gelais & René Audet* tackle two fictional hypertexts: Geoff Ryman's *253* and Rick Pryll's *Lies*. More precisely, they want to critically examine whether fiction should always be approached from the perspective of the narrative. They reject the idea that fiction can be reduced to narrative and that hyperfiction's contribution to textuality is simply the multiplication of possible narratives from a single work. By analyzing *253* and *Lies*, Saint-Gelais and Audet want to get a firmer grip on the narrative expectations of the reader and their necessary reorientation in the face of certain hyperfictions. They show how fictional hypertexts influence the general conception of narrativity precisely because they cannot be reduced to textual jigsaw puzzles or narratives that the reader simply reconstructs in his own way. Without discarding traditional expectations, hyperfiction proposes a reading environment different enough from that of the book so that readers may envisage a renegotiation of the relationship between the support, the discursive organization and the fictional framework – a renegotiation where the computer environment is not reduced to the puzzle-maker's saw but where it contributes on an equal footing, using its own means, to the renewal of both fiction and reading.

In "Stealing or giving" *Jan Baetens* explores the digital materialization of the metaphor of consuming books as eating and reading as cannibalism in Raymond Federman's *Eating Books*, an example of Holocaust fiction profoundly influenced by authors like Beckett and Céline. Baetens rejects the idea that the digital version of a print text cannot be as challenging as one that was initially conceived and elaborated with the new medium in mind. The former is supposed to suffer from its heritage from the print medium – i.e. linearity, passivity and poor use of graphics – as opposed to non-sequentiality, interactivity, and a blurred frontier between the verbal and the visual. *Eating Books*, however, makes use of new media without following the familiar paths. It is deeply rooted in textual culture and does not experiment with spatiality, simultaneity or non-sequentiality. The phonocentric tradition is present through reference to the eating of words and the graphical outline of the work, while the hypertext tradition is strangely absent. Why the work has been transposed from print to new media, however, becomes clear when we think of how new media are supposed to swallow the older media, and steal knowledge like in the anecdote from a London library where Voltaire noticed the presence of a book in the pocket of Newton. Observing that the book seemed to be half-hidden, Voltaire is supposed to have said: "to steal a book is not a crime as long as the book is read."

In "One must be calm and laugh" *Jan Van Looy* investigates how Geoff Ryman's *253* uses hypertext to reflect upon modernity through the thoughts of two hundred and fifty three people in the London Subway. Ryman calls his hyperfiction an Internet Novel, which triggers the question of whether the World Wide Web ought to be considered a medium or a deliverer. The hypertext framework of *253* is highly structured unlike most contemporary hyperfictions, which propagate associative linking from an aesthetic standpoint. Nevertheless, the iconicity of the representation of the train and its passengers plays an important role in the semantics and the narrative development. By molding the narrative space into a rigid hypertextual structure, *253* succeeds in creating a navigational network that reduces cognitive overhead so often experienced in hypertext narrative. The textual space from which meaning is to be deduced is three- instead of two-dimensional. Both hypertextual and narrative syntax are grafted upon the frame story, i.e. an London underground train about to crash. There are several innovative narratological devices at work that together with the way the story is laid out produce a new type of narrative, if it is narrative (see contribution by Saint-Gelais & René Audet). The thematic construction of the novel is based upon both hypertext and narrative structuring and is therefore excellently placed to question its own modernity and that of the narrative world it creates. Decentering, fragmentation and focalization steer the reader through an ingenious type of hyperstory, providing a unique view on modern society through new media.

Cybertext

In *Cybertext: Perspectives on Ergodic Literature* (1997), Espen J. Aarseth introduces the notion of cybertext. Cybertext is a neologism derived from

Norbert Wiener's book (and discipline) called *Cybernetics* and subtitled *Control and Communication in the Animal and the Machine* (1948) (1) and refers to a textual machine or a machine for the production of variety of expression rather than a sequence of signifiers. This machine does not only deliver language or text, but generates signifiers through the manipulation of data arrays, functions, logical operators and programmatic objects. By declaring cybertext a worthwhile object for research, Aarseth expands the realm of literary criticism to a whole range of textual phenomena from short poems to complex computer programs and databases. A cybertext is a device operating on signs; it requires a medium (an interface, the way in which the material is presented to the user, e.g. a workstation, a book) and depends upon the action of a human operator. Thus, it is not only the text produced that is of importance, but also the generation process, or as Ryan describes it: "Computer-modulated texts (poetry machines, cybertexts) are a form of poetry that lives and breathes the fluidity of the electronic environment. They highlight the dynamic production of text, turning this production into a spectacle. Experiencing the text means watching words and meaning emerge and evolve on the screen, animated by the invisible code of a computer program" (Ryan 1999: 9).

The strong mechanical focus of cybertext theory does not mean that the human factor is excluded, that the cyberreader has become a mere slave of the machine. On the contrary, Aarseth claims that the traditional reader is powerless. However strongly engaged, he cannot intervene in the unfolding of the narrative. "Like a spectator at a soccer game, he may speculate, conjecture, extrapolate, even shout abuse, but he is not a player. Like a passenger on a train, he can study and interpret the shifting landscape, he may rest his eyes wherever he pleases, even release the emergency brake and step off, but he is not free to move the tracks in a different direction" (Aarseth 1997: 4). The reader can never experience the pleasure of influence. Rather, it is the pleasure of the voyeur: safe, but impotent. The cybertext reader is not powerless. She can, to a certain extent, change the tracks and score a goal. However, she is not a safe reader; she suffers the risk of rejection. "The effort and energy demanded by the cybertext of its reader raise the stakes of interpretation to those of intervention" (4). Thus computer-generated literature becomes a process of collaboration between man and machine automatically resulting in three possible positions: the computer as pre-processor, co-processor and post-processor.

The configuration in which the computer is pre-processor can best be illustrated by traditional artificial intelligence in which the computer generates an outline or blueprint for the human partner, who can then translate it into literary language. Typical examples for this category are story-generating programs developed in the seventies and eighties as contributions to artificial intelligence research. (The best known is *Tale-spin* by James Meehan.) "What matters in these projects is not their output *per se* – usually mediocre imitations of standard types of narrative such as fables or fairy tales – but the reasoning power of the generative algorithm and its credibility as a simulation of human creative processes" (Ryan 1999: 2). A typical example of the computer as co-processor is *ELIZA*, a computer program that simulates a Rogerian therapist written by Joseph Weizenbaum in 1966. Again, the primary focus is not to produce literature, but rather to test the conversational capabilities of computer programs (3). Finally, the computer as post-processor manipulates a text produced by a human author. The texts belonging to this category are not related to artificial intelligence research. Textual fragments are handled as opaque objects, not as meaning bearing units to form a sort of experimental, dynamic, literature. "A computer program fabricates text out of ready-made texts by searching a database for elements fitting certain patterns (rhymes, palindromes, and anagrams) or by subjecting the input text(s) to various aleatory procedures, such as collage and permutations." (4).

While the traditional reader only performs in his head, the user of cybertext performs in the literal sense. During cybertextual dialogue, she effectuates a semiotic sequence involving an activity of physical construction which can impossibly be accounted for just by the concept of 'reading'. This phenomenon Aarseth calls ergodic, using a term appropriated from physics that derives from the Greek words ergon and hodos, meaning 'work' and 'path'. "In ergodic literature, nontrivial effort is required to allow the reader to traverse the text" (Aarseth 1997: 1). Ergodic textuality has existed for as long as linear writing. To exemplify this, Aarseth refers to the wall inscriptions of temples in ancient Egypt, which were often connected two-dimensionally (on one wall) or three-dimensionally (from wall to wall and from room to room). This layout allowed a nonlinear arrangement of the religious text in accordance with the symbolic architectural layout of the temple (9). Probably the best-known example of cybertext in antiquity is the *I Ching* or the *Book of Changes* (1122-770 b.c.), which inspired Leibniz while developing binary mathematics. Another prototypical example is Raymond Queneau's *Cent Mille Milliards de Poèmes* (a hundred thousand billion poems; see Queneau 1961), which is a sonnet machine book of 10 x 14 lines, capable of producing 10^{14} sonnets (10). However, cybertextuality is not an isolated phenomenon; it is a perspective on all forms of textuality which permits to expand literary studies to phenomena that have been hitherto marginalized. Using seven variables (dynamics, determinability, transiency, perspective, access, linking and user functions)

Aarseth describes texts, ranging from Herman Melville's *Moby Dick* (1851) to John Cayley's *Book Unbound* (1995) according to their mode of traversal.

In the first essay of the cybertext section *Jack Post* analyzes the Web site Darren Aronofsky created for his film *Requiem for a dream*. Post uses the perspective of Johanna Drucker's theory on the aesthetics of typography to demonstrate with great limpidity how we can profit from a critical return to Hjelmslev, whose theory provides the necessary theoretical basis for approaching the materiality in language and multimedia practices. Since the success of *The Blair Witch Project*, in which its Web site played a decisive role, it has become clear that new media can be an important extension for films. While most of these Web sites simply provide a gallery of images, a synopsis of the story and sometimes background information on the actors, Aronofsky chose a radically different approach. Like the film, the Web site is meant to be an experience onto itself, an independent complement to the film. Instead of creating a billboard, Aronofsky and Florian Schmitt, the designer of the site, strove to design something that reflects the tone of the film in the new medium. The theme of addiction is laid out and commented upon in visual cybertext. Greimas and Courtès' semiotic theory serves to underpin the analysis of the *Requiem for a dream* Web site as a poetic text. The 'reader' of this type of cybertext can be described as a bundle of various 'readings' corresponding with the different semiotic systems or forms actualized in a syncretic text.

Paul A. Harris's essay starts as a discussion of the ways a database structure modifies the nature of narrative in hyperfiction, but soon the scope of the article shifts to the narrative of an interface. Harris deals with the discussion on the redesign and conceptual transformation of the *electronic book review* (ebr) interface. He plays with the fact that he is writing a print essay about electronic text. This duality is both the theme of the essay and the object under investigation. By describing how ideas for the new interface occur, transform and finally materialize, he comments on how the electronic medium is subject to both material and conceptual design. His account of how a virtual community shares knowledge and experience in order to jointly produce a new way of looking at, and presenting the content of an electronic journal, is highly refreshing. The initial concept of the ebr Web site needed serious rethinking in the light of new ideas on the cultural contradictions between old an new media, and the emergence of "multi-course" (a term coined by Hayles which alludes both to multiple discourse and to the multiple reading paths made possible by hypertext). The result of the process is not static form delivering the required content, but a recursive dynamic whole in which Web sites and hypermedia works embed narrative elements within a linked structure, the design principles of which then come to shape and become an integral part of the narrative content – which in turn may effect reconceptions in the design as the work unfolds.

In the final contribution of this volume, *Mark Amerika* revisits the *Grammatron* doxa in an attempt to come to terms with what he calls 'hypertextual consciousness', "the advent of a new stage, perhaps the final one, in the political, spiritual, and artistic growth of mankind" (Ryan 2001: 8). Starting with 'another memex moment' he alphabetically wanders through the conceptual space of contemporary new media theory. In some fifty entries he describes and illustrates his views on what Internet, virtual reality, art and reading could and should be. With one foot in the present and two eyes on the future, he explores 'play' both in its poststructuralist and commonsense meaning. He is constantly searching for an adequate set of tools for structuring, analyzing and conceptualizing electronic literature of today and tomorrow. He sings the praises of the eventual liberation of the mind from the body, of text from the book and of youth from their television set. In a highly evocative style Amerika creates images of what could and perhaps will be. His words and sentences thump like techno beats while thoughts and ideas jump into new constellations. By using the dictionary format, he attempts to linearize and order hypertextual consciousness into a story on the verge of chaos. He intermingles powerful theoretical images with fictional examples tributary to William Gibson. In this way, hypertextual consciousness becomes a dream-narrative application, an always already applied grammatology, the science of writing teleported into cyberspace, the world's revenge on television.

Works cited

Aarseth, Espen J. (1997). *Cybertext: Perspectives on Ergodic Literature*. Baltimore, London: The Johns Hopkins University Press.
Barthes, Roland (1974). *S/Z*. New York: Hill and Wang.
Berners-Lee Tim (2000). "Frequently Asked Questions". <http://www.w3.org/People/Berners-Lee/FAQ.html>
Birkerts, Sven (1994). *The Gutenberg Elegies: the Fate of Reading in an Electronic Age*. New York: Fawcett Columbine.
Bolter, Jay David & Grusin, Richard (1999). *Remediation: Understanding New Media*. Cambridge, Massachusetts: The MIT Press.
Bush, Vannevar (1945). "As We May Think" in *The Atlantic Monthly* July 1945 Volume 176, No1; 101-108. Boston: The Atlantic Monthly Group.
Cavell, Stanley (1979). *The world Viewed. Enlarged Edition*. Cambridge, Mass.: Harvard University Press.

— (1981). *Pursuits of happiness: the Hollywood comedy of remarriage.* Cambridge, Mass.: Harvard University Press.
Cayley, John (1995). *Book Unbound.* London: Wellsweep.
Cortazar, Julio (1966). *Hopscotch.* New York: Avon Books.
Derrida, Jacques (1967). *De la Grammatologie.* Paris: Editions de Minuit.
Fontanille, Jacques(1999). "Préface", in Alain Vuillemin and Michel Lenoble (eds.), *Littérature, Informatique, Lecture. De la lecture assistée par ordinateur à la lecture interactive.* Limoges: Pulim, pp. I-VIII.
Gaggi, Silvio (1997). *From text to hypertext: decentering the subject in fiction, film, the visual arts, and electronic media.* Philadelphia, Pa.: University of Pennsylvania Press.
Joyce, Michael (1990). *Afternoon, A Story.* Electronic text. Watertown, PA: Eastgate, 1990.
Keep, Christopher & McLaughlin, Tim & Parmar, Robin (1995). *The Electronic Labyrinth,* <http://jefferson.village.virginia.edu/elab/hfl0098.html>.
Landow, George P. *Hypertext 2.0: The Convergence of Contemporary Critical Theory and Technology.* Baltimore: John Hopkins UP, 1997.
Manovich, Lev (2001). *The Language of New Media.* Cambridge, Massachusetts: The MIT Press.
Meehan, James R. (1977). "TALE-SPIN, An Interactive Program that Writes Stories" in Reddy, R. *Proceedings of the 5th International Joint Conference on Artificial Intelligence.* Cambridge, MA, August 1977.
Melville, Herman (1851). *Moby Dick; or, The Whale.* London.
Moulthrop, Stuart (1991) *Victory Garden.* Electronic text. Watertown, MA: Eastgate Systems.
Nelson, Theodor Holm (1965). "A File Structure for the Complex, the Changing, and the Indeterminate." In *Proceedings of the 20th National Conference,* 84-100. New York: Association for Computing Machinery.
— (1974). *Computer Lib/Dream Machines.* Redmond: Tempus Books.
— (1993 [1981]) *Literary Machines.* Sausalito, CA: Mindful Press.
Queneau, Raymond (1961). *Cent mille milliards de poèmes.* Paris: Gallimard.
Ryan, Marie-Laure, ed. (1999). *Cyberspace Textuality: Computer Technology and Literary Theory.* Bloomington: Indiana University Press.
— (2001). *Narrative as Virtual Reality: Immersion and Interactivity in Literature and Electronic Media.* Baltimore and London: The Johns Hopkins University Press.
Turkle, Sherry (1995). *Life on the Screen: Identity in the Age of the Internet.* New York: Simon & Schuster.
Van Looy, Jan (forthcoming). "Uneasy lies the head that wears a crown: interactivity and signification in *Head Over Heels*" in Game Studies <http://www.gamestudies.org>.
Weizenbaum, Joseph (1966). *ELIZA.* Computer Program. Several versions available on the Internet.
Wiener, Norbert (1948). *Cybernetics; or, Control and Communication in the Animal and the Machine.* New York: Technology Press.
Wolfreys, Julian (2000). *Readings: Acts of close reading in literary theory.* Edinburgh: Edinburgh University Press.

I
Hypertext

Stephanie Strickland's *True North*: A Migration between Media

Joseph Tabbi
(University of Illinois - Chicago)

One poem, two media – a book, and a disk. In Stephanie Strickland's winter migration from print to electronic text (Strickland 1997/1998), we can observe the forces that are transforming literary culture, and its study, in our time. Frequently in *True North*, Strickland makes reference – and hypertext may be, even in poetry, primarily a medium and method of annotation – to Muriel Rukeyser's 1942 biography of Josiah Willard Gibbs (1839-1903). From this source comes the narration of an incident, of a sort to help posterity recognize a man "of whom," says Rukeyser, "so few stories have been told" (224):

> Gibbs spoke only once
> in a Faculty Meeting, during
> protracted, tiring debate on elective courses:
> should there be – more English, more Classics? More? Or less.
> They were astonished to see him rise, after thirty-two years,
> though familiar with the high, pained-sounding voice: a man of snow
> assessing. Not to be distracted, or dispersed into longcuts,
> not to be turned from the whole entire empty mist
> hanging in the cold air, not to miss – or
> intrude on the nothing that was
> there.
>
> Escaping
> in every emotional way,
> Gibbs, hidden at home, creating the loneliness
> he needed to assume just one responsibility – for which no thanks,
> much complaining of it, some wonder. Lost, in the clouds of snow gathering
> in CT over Transactions & Proceedings of the local Academy of Sciences,
> the one un-evasion he accepted: shortcutting elegance by uncouth
> statement that is efficient in every respect. The reward for
> getting past the failings of language? To be found
> un-readable. Gibbs rose. He said: Mathematics
> is a language. And sat down.
> (Strickland 1997: 61)

"Never married, never moved from their Family Home," more at home with ideas than with people: like another recurring presence in *True North*, Emily Elizabeth Dickinson (1830-1886), Gibbs would seem "As alive,/ or more so, in the grave as out of it" (48). Dickinson writes of dwelling in possibility; her persona, characteristically speaking in "The clipped and polite cadence of a caller's speech" (Rukeyser 1942: 175), can be heard in *True North* as if from "across the garden/ fence of the grave":

> Speaking in the tomb, of the tomb, as of a ride,
> one of many, every poem one of many, No-name inquiries –
> (Strickland 1997: 48)

A poem takes a singular form on the page or on the screen, but meaning depends on redundancy and the repetition of patterns internally and in other poems, both written and unwritten, published and (in Dickinson's case) "stitched into" private notebooks (Strickland 1997: 40). Having few stories to tell, at the risk of unreadability, poetry approaches a generality usually reserved for the non-referential arts – music and mathematics. Gibbs's "700/ equations/ /...set up in type at last/ by shopkeepers'/ subscription" (Strickland 1997: 40) approximate the state of a thermodynamic system not by describing the system itself or narrating its actual history, but by reference to all possible states, the various ways in which its elements arrange themselves as the system evolves. A prediction was never more than an approximation, to be corrected and re-drawn through continual comparison with the real state of the system (meaning "any portion of the universe which we choose to separate in thought, in order to consider it" [Rukeyser 1942: 235]). In Connecticut, "they/ Make Do": the mode of publication, the material form by which the work of Gibbs and Dickinson was given to their initial audiences, establishes a pattern that – so far from being incidental to the "meaning" of a poem or equation – in some sense determines the possibility of all future meanings, as the poem or equation finds various and usually unanticipated material instantiations.

A "hotword" in hypertext at once identifies an emerging pattern in one system and allows entry into another; three such words appear in the paragraph just concluded: system, prediction, history. Although it takes us too far from the subject at hand here, I would contend that there are a number of distinct and indeed incompatible historicist trajectories in Marx's own work. Many of these historicist projections turned out to be wrong. But that was precisely the point of them. In the difference between the trajectory plotted by a historicist theory and the wayward movements of history itself lies a method which allows for a constant writing and rewriting of the pleasures and dangers of the future. (McKenzie 1994: 223-24)

The introduction of the new in poetry – the 'really new', as T.S. Eliot might have said – requires a re-adjustment of all the mental categories by which we have come to know and recognize poetry as such. (Eliot's word for the set of categories facilitating poetic re/cognition was "tradition.") Strickland's poetics of indirect citation, annotation, and recombination creates affinities with a distinctive (and mostly American) tradition that reaches back through Dickinson to Jonathan Edwards. Her willingness to court abstraction and a minimalist language (at the risk of occasional unreadability) opens what should be a fruitful conversation with the Language Poets, while the recognition awarded *True North* by the judges for the Sandeen Prize ensures that her work will be welcomed into the domestic spaces of contemporary social realism no less than the more public-minded collectivities represented at meetings of the Modern Language Association and the Society for Literature and Science (where Strickland has given readings). A contemporary of Gibbs whom Rukeyser, for some reason, identifies only as "Kraus," gives the most useful appreciation of the particular mix of intellection and materialist attention in Strickland's poetry. A member of the Yale Department of Physics, Kraus left in its archives an evaluation of an early invention by Gibbs, "a new type of governor" constructed locally in the outlying shops of industrial New Haven. What Kraus writes concerning a scientist known almost exclusively for his contributions to theory is equally suggestive for readers with an interest in the role of theory in literary invention:

> "Until we have come to know that Gibbs was endowed with a mind which possessed a keen appreciation of and interest in things physical and practical, his life and works remain a profound mystery. Possessing intellectual powers of the highest order, as much at home in pure mathematics as in physics and chemistry, Gibbs constantly exercised his will to direct his thoughts along lines that lay within the framework of material phenomena." (cited in Rukeyser 1942: 144-45)

Gibbs's media, and the sociological meaning of his work, were given to him by the ruling industrialists of the last third of the last century; his theory is materialist not because it reduces the world to brute fact, but rather because its abstractions find expression in processes and inventions that would only later be actualized, through a material world that on closer inspection increasingly "mists away into mystical refinements" (Ammons 1993: 25). I suspect that, behind Strickland's decision to publish

True North as both a conventional print collection and a hypertext, lies something of this desire to exercise power by directing language and thought through the time's defining media (and, through models that are never more than approximations, to rewrite our understanding of "the pleasures and dangers of the future" [Wark 1994: 224]). Two-part publication does not mean that Strickland simply put the print version of the manuscript on disk (as in those CD-ROMs, published by Norton and others, whose engagement with the medium is purely quantitative, the next step after it becomes impossible to make the paper in anthologies any thinner). Electronic publication should never be a simple process of conversion. Strickland's achievement is to locate the poetic possibilities inherent in the new medium, such that imagination might find expression in tags and numbers and nested programs no less than in words.[1] Making do with materials that stand ready to hand, "American Artificers" find "Articula[tion] Among Us" and a distinctively "American Speech" (to cite, somewhat inaccurately, three titles in the section of *True North* featuring Gibbs and Dickinson). In a hypertext poem whose lines can be linked together unpredictably into suggestive patterns, the line itself – as a figure – becomes a primary source of articulation:

> a slow
> > seep into melting snow and gray afternoon;
> > > Gibby, skating
>
> long strokes on the pond; Emily
> > watching freedom
> > > condense
>
> inside the clear glass of her window.
> > In this Valley, neighbors
> > > disregard
>
> - sustain - hidden fervence, run Underground
> > railroads; Images and Shadows
> > > sewn up

---

[1] On her motivations for working in the new medium, Strickland writes, "I think that I was seeking to write hypertext – not knowing what I was looking for then – all the way back as far as trying to deal with Simone Weil's life and thought, a case where she had no authority over publication of her own work. One was faced with making do with a variety of false, because madly partisan, accounts – the interpretive paradigms are at such odds with each other, but all apply. *True North* explores guidance and navigation/orientation when *these* are very much up for grabs. All the candidate answers however use some basic bodily metaphors in their language, and pregnancy, which gets read as containment, embedding, self-similarity, subsethood, etc. in different contexts, is certainly one of the basic metaphors explored in *TN*, a central mother-lost category as pregnancy becomes removed from the body to the laboratory vessel" (private correspondence, December 17, 1998).

> in Edwards's notebooks, flint
>   stitched into Dickinson's, 700
>   equations
>
> of Gibbs's great paper set up in type at last
>   by shopkeepers'
>   subscription: in CT, they
>
> Make Do, but they tore
>   the house, the home on High Street, Gibbs's – born
>   and died there - down.
> (Strickland 1997: 39-40)

This poem – "American Speech" – elaborates a network of curving lines and stitched threads but ends in a single downward stroke, recalling Gibbs's return to his seat after speaking up at the Yale faculty meeting. Whether presenting a formula for the phase transformation from ice to water (which happens as the boy Gibbs describes literal lines on ice while skating), following the thread of Dickinson's sewing needle, or tracing a network of individual flights from racial and political oppression ("American Speech" begins with the line, "Resistance to tyrants is obedience to God" [39]), Strickland is generally reflecting on the poetic 'line' and its potential inscriptions (i.e., how it gets written down) in print and on disk.

"It's Easy," Strickland writes, "at the South Pole. There every/ direction/ is true North....every,/ and so easy,/ at/ /the nadir" (83). Actual techniques of determining true north using stake, shadow, and turning ground are detailed in a series of five one-page poems that come between sections, facilitating transitions among them. (The five titles are colored true blue in the hypertext; the electronic links both forward and backward from each inter-poem to the poems collected in sections, make this mediating function easier in hypertext than in print.) In seeking control and direction, and by asserting force ("...anyone/ coming forward to speak/ is using force" [15]), a network of feminine possibility (which "can only/ stand waiting, here/ on earth, where// there are no/ straight/ lines" [15]) collapses in a downward and Southern reduction, ending (for the transcendentalist Edwards) in a single act of perception, a marriage of subject and object in the presiding male consciousness "at the breast of the whitening world" (53):

> In CT, waves of wet snow, in waves
> of gravitation. Receiving the vision,
> Mathema-physics, Locke's psychology,
>
> the Universe Organized around
> an act of mind: the knowable confined
> to the reach of lengthening instrumentation
>
> and the mind's self-knowing and their inter-
> penetration. If God had left off speaking,
> once code was stated, briefly,

> then Rhetoric should too. The tangible
> world intaken: intelligible. The fact
> of experience, a shadow of God: the act
>
> of cognition a moment of fusion in which
> a thing finds its concept - and is found.
> This is a mind of snow in Connecticut.
>
> This is a Snow Mind knowing as if None
> knew. Exhilarated. Brilliant. An eagle
> at the breast of the whitening world.
>   (Strickland 1997: 53)

The emotional reduction that Gibbs the Puritan made of his life, and the material reduction that defines his abstract, minimalist, and eventually forceful science, are both ways of cultivating a "Snow mind knowing as if None/ knew." An unassuming man by nature, Gibbs succeeded in creating an abstract science largely, according to Rukeyser, by keeping to a minimum the number of assumptions made about the physical world. It would be left to later generations of scientists – most dramatically, Planck, Einstein, and the computer scientists – to bring out the power inherent in the 700 equations summarizing Gibbs's lifework. The theorist offers orientations only; discerning practical power in the theory is slow work indeed, involving constant comparisons and approximations that Strickland compares to a journey across the earth's sphere. "[O]n earth... //there are no/ straight/ lines" (15): but at the South, the nadir, "the breast of the whitening world," every direction is potentially a longitude, a great circle path north. There is imagined fecundity in potentia – until one takes the first step: after that, as potential collapses into a single actualization, the explorer must compare her position with the place where she started, exchanging self-reliance for a dependence on measurement – in this case, using the simplest, most sustainable technology available, a stick and its shadow. Later actualizations, employing more complex technologies, not even a Gibbs could have predicted.

> Each of the five major episodes [of mass extinction]... represents a drastic net loss of species
> diversity, a deep trough of biological impoverishment from which Earth only slowly recovered. How
> slowly? How long is the lag between a nadir of impoverishment and a recovery to ecological fullness?
>   (Quammen 1998: 58)

The feminine stitchwork in a book's binding, though seldom noticed, adds a rotational dimension to the act of reading, making codex technology less obviously "linear" than one might think. By the same token, reading poems has always evoked a kind of flickering or oscillating attention that hypertext reinforces, by foregrounding formal connections and verbal juxtapositions, and by inviting readers to jump to another poem as readily as they might go on to the next line in the poem they are reading. Clickable links which display on command (using the ctrl key) connect every poem to as many as six or seven other poems, and colored words suggesting subliminal connections, keep within the reader's consciousness the many levels at which meaning must work. Reading Strickland, I am inclined to read around in the collection and, eventually, to go outside it – to books such as Rukeyser's that Strickland cites (and so renews), and to books and articles that, while perhaps unknown to the poet and incidental to her line of thought, at some collective level help to realize potentialities arrived at privately and recorded in the poem.

I am inclined, for example, to look up the preface to *The Human Use of Human Beings: Cybernetics and Society*, in which Norbert Wiener discusses Gibbs's deviations from linear thinking – "the first great revolution of twentieth century physics" – in terms that should by now suggest a pattern of thought reminiscent of hypertext reading. Wiener writes: "...in a probabilistic world we no longer deal with... a specific, real universe as a whole [as in the Newtonian model of the universe] but ask instead questions which may find their answers in a large number of similar universes.... Gibbs' innovation was to consider not one world, but all the worlds which are possible answers to a limited set of questions concerning our environment. His central notion concerned the extent to which answers that we may give to questions about one set of worlds are probable among a larger set of worlds. (Wiener 1954: 18-19, 20)

Writing six years before Wiener, Rukeyser transposed Gibbs's innovation into literary terms, so that the uneventful 'life' comes to us as one variation on many possible lives. Rukeyser, who according to Strickland "fought for his biography" against "cohorts of colleagues and family" (Strickland 1997: 41), does not focus on the isolation Gibbs cultivated, but instead narrates a series of relations, counterparts, and corresponding points. An amateur in thermodynamics writing too early to be influenced directly by computers, Rukeyser expresses both through a nested narrative; periodically, she allows the line of Gibbs's life and thought to be broken by modular narratives of other lives and modes of thought that impinged on his: James Clerk Maxwell in Cambridge, the first to understand him; Henry Adams, William James, and Charles Sanders Peirce of Harvard University who, like Gibbs at Yale in 1871, founded disciplines by combining areas of knowledge previously thought distinct – experimental psychology for James, a dynamic theory of history for Adams, semiotics for Peirce, and, in Gibbs's case, mathematical physics and statistical mechanics. This biography constructed of counterparts and correlations is far richer and ultimately more human than those biographies – standard today – whose authors insist on narrating a life as if it amounted to an intelligible "story." The universe that had formed him took shape in his mind as a reflection of his own unity, containing all forces except himself. (Adams 1961: 475)

In *True North*, Rukeyser's life of Gibbs is seen for what it wasn't seen to be at the time of its publication, a new kind of history. It serves Strickland less as an information source or cultural reference-point than a model of mind, and this becomes, in another of *True North*'s unravelling references, Wallace Stevens's "mind of winter" aware of "Nothing that is not there and the nothing that is" (cited in Strickland 1997: 61). In the electronic version of Strickland's poem published by Eastgate Systems, clicking on this epigraph from "The Snow Man" takes me to the next poem in the section, titled "Natural Numbers" and subheaded with an empty set of parentheses: ( ). A pattern of nested parentheses – (( ), ((( )), etc. – is then developed in subheadings for each of the subsequent poems in the section (six altogether), ending in a pattern that contains in reverse order the first two letters of the section titles, "Natural," "Integral," "Rational," "Real," "(Imaginary)":

(IM   (RE (RA   (IN   (NA   )))).

(The pattern reverses the order of poems, but this is the correct logical order for embedding numbers on the number line, where the category for "imaginary" numbers contains the "real," contains "rational," contains "integers" etc.).[2] That's one possible trajectory through the section – a linear reading that makes explicit reference to "embedded links that connect embodied experience with universal abstraction" (in the words of N. Katherine Hayles cited on the book jacket).

But that's not the thread I'm following at the moment, in this reading which is one of many readings that Eastgate's software can capture and save for future recall. I am interested, instead, in pursuing the Stevens reference, insofar as it concentrates a number of themes already noted in Strickland's winter migration. Lines in the e-text referring to a "storm/ in the night so great,/ so erasing the man" are not given as clickable links leading out to other poems in the collection. Nonetheless, traditional habits of

---

[2] Strickland elaborates: "Also that pattern, becoming verbal and thereby changing levels, changes levels again when it moves from an acronym to a name, Im Re.Rainna: Im Re.writing (I'm Rerainna, I'm rewriting...) "She" is the author. Of what, the book, the hypertext, the endeavor? Or another lost mother who writes from the communal oral experiential side, shifting the levels? Or akin to Adam Smith's hand?" (private correspondence, Dec 17, 1998.)

reading suffice for generating resonances, affinities, and recurrences in any number of passages on snow in Connecticut:

> Gibbs making found
>
>> what lies hidden, so deeply nested
>> is it within, so down
>> deeply pocketed, miles
>
>> from the icy, calm, notational
>> surface: making a line,
>> a lure, one symbol, one elliptical
>
>> expression, holding echo
>> upon echo, decoding
>> to a catalog: an infinite
>
>>> acceptance...
>
> detonation
>
>> as almost welcome and always
>> implicit
>> in the mind, like the cloud, low
>> and going to snow
>> in CT. Great still pool. Demoralized
>> desire that waits for
>> snow
>> as if the snow were
>
>>> winged
>
> (Strickland 1997: 51)

"Demoralise," we learn elsewhere, is "...the one/ word/ /Noah Webster invented, of all those/ in his book" (39). This one word, spelled with an English "s" by Webster but used with a current z in the later occurrence, is an example of the embedded and subliminal way that Strickland tracks history. "Demoralise" is a clickable link in the hypertext version, but clicking on it does not lead, mechanically, to the place where it recurs (as "Demoralized"). A hypertext poetics need not automate interpretation and had better not offer links in place of reading habits that can only be cultivated in the mind of a practiced reader. Poetry is better served through indirection. In this case, the hypertext link demoralise is tagged to the title of the opening section of *True North*, "The Mother-Lost World." Once there, five or six poems into the section, a highlighted reference to TechnI.con(tm), "a patented genomic sac," leads to a poem titled "Pregnancy," while the word "stainless" leads to another poem that speaks of what "science/ creates." Two other words, "fatal" and the last two syllables in "precursor," are highlighted in the same purple as TechnI.con(tm). These also are tagged to "Pregnancy," which speaks of cell migrations, undulations, and "layered movement" that science has yet to understand. In this context, technology's own stumbling efforts at evolution, and science's less destructive efforts at knowing, are themselves contextualized as elements in the poem's organic and layered processes.

What is demoralizing about all this is the idea of how much has been lost by the many mothers in this poem. Just as much as the Puritanical ascetic abstract quest demoralizes (and strengthens) men such as Edwards and Peirce and Adams and Gibbs, there is demoralization in the lost potential embodied by the various women in the collection. Among all the lost mothers of the Mother-Lost world – Mother Goose, the old woman of Beare, Briseis "Found/ in bed, aborted" (Strickland 1997: 8), Eve, the Witch of Endor, and Dickens's Mme. DeFarge (whose knitting, like Dickinson's, holds structural secrets) – I have to include the author in the process of organizing the final text out of elements that had another life, in earlier publishing contexts, before they were deployed into the recombinant space of the Eastgate *True North*.

One way – a traditionalist way – of psychologizing these dichotomies between male force and female fecundity, technology and science, is through an implied tension between a desire and a lack. Throughout True North, an impulse toward naming (identified with a masculine fulfillment that collapses potential) and a loss of reference (conveyed, for the most part, through feminine associations of disorientation and Eve-like wanting to know), combine together toward the same downward thrust (made visible, this time, in the shape of the lines):

> A lover who eschews force – anyone
> coming forward to speak
> is using force -
>
> can only
> stand waiting, here
> on earth, where
>
> there are no
> straight
> lines

(Strickland 1997: 15)

For Stevens thinking about what it means to be human, consciousness and its powers of delineation emerge from precisely such an absence or a lack – a nothing that is both there and not there, an observed universe that contains all forces but the observing self. But Strickland, in her arrangement of lines, does more than recite the thought structures of a major modernist precursor. The differential basis of this structure, familiar in philosophers from Plato to Derrida, is the hierarchy between presence and absence, by which "presence is aligned with logos, God, teleology – in general, with an originary plenitude that can act to ground signification and give order and meaning to the trajectory of history" (Hayles, *How We Became Posthuman*, 285). Between "the fact/ of experience" and "the act/ /of cognition," the explorer – Edwards, Gibbs, Pythagoras in his quest for Real numbers – seeks a ground in which "a thing finds its concept," and then, Godlike, he leaves off speaking (Strickland 1997: 53).

With this traditionalist formulation, I am perhaps ready to leave Stevens and take up the alternative thread through Strickland's poem suggested by Professor Hayles, who sees new ways of thinking emerging in part from the development of electronic media and their grounding in information theory (whose practitioners have traveled some distance in the years since Wiener named the field cybernetics and identified it with the study of systems of control). Hayles characterizes the "new cultural configurations" as developing out of a simple "shift from presence/absence to pattern/randomness" (285). Such emergent form is evident everywhere in Strickland's sequence of poems, but nowhere is it better illustrated, perhaps, than in the cover art for the print version by Joseph Cornell, titled *Constellation (Project for a Christmas Card)* (1953). Painted against a dark cardboard background are paper lines, straight and curved, and spattered points that perhaps resemble a snowstorm, a field of stars, or (looked at coldly) particle traces in a bubble chamber. Perched on one of the lines, also in white but with some of the dark background showing through, is a cutout picture of a bird in profile, beak to the right. The human image (and the bird is drawn as only a human, most likely a child, would imagine it) emerges out of an abstract and random set of forces; it is a gnomon or orientation device in a directionless space, where the concept of 'north' is wholly abstract.

Such is the visual language of the poem. Verbally, in the poem's own medium, we can approach the emergence of pattern from randomness in a line Strickland attributes to Gibbs's father, "Josiah Willard, the Elder, Professor at Yale/ of sacred books": "Language/ /is a cast of the human mind" (46). The father's words combine with the son's singular declaration before the Yale faculty: "Mathematics/ is a language." Against the fecundity, passivity, and random noise of the Mother-Lost world, True North also delineates an intellectual progression in the development of abstract knowledge. Not a linear progression and not an opposition among conflicting stances. Instead, the poem creates in the mind of the reader a disposition, while reading, to combine recurrent phrases in a sidelong or Web-like fashion: Mathematics is a Language is a Cast of the Human Mind... Phrases already formed are likewise broken down and defamiliarized, as in the title, "Even Purits Forced to Re-Cog." Cognition becomes a matter of cogs and counterparts. A modular mind of winter, consciousness is stripped "naked" so as to better combine with structures that emerge from background noise – from the electrical snow that is the only ground of meaning, the background source of any positive communication of information.

Language is a cast: it seeks fixity and gives shape through a set form; it also generates meaning out of randomness, as in the throw of a die. Or the flinging of a fishing line.

At the start of this essay, in passing, I identified literary hypertext as, in the first instance, a technology of annotation. One should not take this to imply a passive citation of an authoritative source. Rather, the hypertextual citation is a means of releasing the power of established forms by placing them in new contexts, where they may combine in ways (and through media) not necessarily foreseen by those who created the forms initially. In closing, I ought to perhaps mention one technical feature of True North that works to limit that propensity towards out-of-context citation and recombination. Eastgate has made it impossible to copy a poem simply by passing the cursor over the text, thus inhibiting the freedom of citation and Web circulation that hypertext ought to be encouraging. One can of course copy the disk onto other machines, in toto, but however wide its reproduction, the electronic poem is restricted to a single location – the publisher's disk and the owner's hard-drive – more or less as the print collection is restricted to the bound pages of a book. If this prevents the text from escaping the control of the author and her publisher, nothing keeps readers from completing its recombinant aesthetic in the privacy of their own minds, as readers have done for as long as they've been singled out as consumers.

Works cited

Adams, Henry (1961). *The Education of Henry Adams* (1918). Boston: Houghton Mifflin.
Ammons, A.R (1993). *Garbage*. New York: Norton.
Hayles, N. Katherine (1999). *How We Became Posthuman: Virtual Bodies in Cybernetics, Literature, and Infomatics*. Chicago: University of Chicago Press.
McKenzie Wark (1994), *Virtual Geography*. Bloomington: Indiana University Press.
Quammen, David (1998). "Planet of Weeds: Tallying the losses of Earth's animals and plants." *Harper's Magazine* (October, 1998): 57-69.
Rukeyser, Muriel (1942). *Willard Gibbs*. New York: Doubleday, Doran & Company.
Strickland, Stephanie (1997). *True North*. Notre Dame, IN: Notre Dame University Press.
— (1998). *True North*. Electronic text. Watertown, MA: Eastgate Systems.
Wark, McKenzie (1994). *Virtual Geography: Living with Global Media Events*. Bloomington: Indiana University Press.
Wiener, Norbert (1954). *The Human Use of Human Beings: Cybernetics and Society* (2nd ed.). Garden City, NY: Doubleday.

Sutured Fragments:
Shelley Jackson's *Patchwork Girl* in Piecework

Elisabeth Joyce
(Edinboro University of Pennsylvania)

Recent theoretical approaches to cultural studies have taken the map as a metaphor for the body and as an analogy of the impress of cultural structures on geographical space as well as on the subjectivity of the individual.[1] Shelley Jackson's *Patchwork Girl* (Eastgate, 1995) depicts the urge to define space through the grid of the map on three levels: hypertextual, narratal and corporeal.[2] Its form as a hypertext forces it to identify the passage through the text as the movement along the axis of mapping. Each sector of the work lays out its network of pages in a successive manner, just as a map indicates the order, length, and links of roads to a destination. This hypertext's map even presents the differentiation between the portions of the text in terms of the map's labeling and color patterns. The grid of this map is misleading, though, because it purports to establish a clear and logical route through the hypertext, but following that route leads the reader no closer to a linear narrative than a more haphazardly selected series of links do.[3] Even by taking the map's indicated directions, the links from page to page disrupt the narrative, creating a text based on random interlocking fragments.

---

[1] Among these are *Mind and Body Spaces: Geographies of Ilness, Impairment and Disability*, Ruth Butler and Hester Parr (New York: Routledge, 1999); *Places through the Body*, Heidi Nast and Steven Pile (New York: Routledge, 1998); and *Body- and Image-Space: Re-reading Walter Benjamin*, Sigrid Weigel (New York: Routledge, 1997).
[2] Relatively few essays have been written on this hypertext to date, but the one by Katharine Hayles is quite extensive.
[3] Michael Joyce relates the passage through a hypertext to "how the reader in motion across the space of a text inhabits a map not as a map but as the rereading of a map which we enact in (and as) our bodies," p. 588.

The text emphasizes this dislocation of narrative sequence through its appropriation of texts, primarily from Mary Shelley's *Frankenstein*, but also from Frank Oz's *The Patchwork Girl of Oz*, Barbara Maria Stafford's *Body Criticism: Imaging the Unseen in Enlightenment Art and Medicine*, and others. The incorporation of these texts into the narrative serves to snap the threads of the linear progression of a plot, rupturing repeatedly the reader's efforts to piece together the story.

The third mapping level of this hypertext relates to the body of the girl herself. Just as Dr. Frankenstein sews together the monster's body from body parts gleaned from corpses, this girl's body is an appropriation of human remains, each fragment still imbued with the character of its original owner. Because of this co-mingling of others' organs and limbs, the Patchwork Girl has no clear identity. The sections of her body will not remain sutured together, frayed constantly by the dissonance of the first owners' characters, as well as by the disjuncture of the narrative and of the hypertext itself. Even so, the subjectivity of this "quilted" figure may finally be accurate from the perspective of theories of identity like those of Gilles Deleuze and Felix Guattari. If, as they suggest, identity is more a concatenation of multiplicities than a coherently unified block of self, then perhaps the patchwork girl is as stitched together as any of the rest of us: a threadbare lacework of taut threads. The body then becomes a corporate entity, a collective unit, and a map of its components then becomes a mere representation of its layers and patterns that adhere in the final form of the mosaic of its subjectivity.[4]

Mapping

Four different kinds of mapping structures are available on Storyspace, the software program on which Jackson composed Patchwork Girl: the map, the chart, the outline and the tree map.[5] Each map style depicts the layout of the hypertext in a different manner, setting up the chapters as headings and identifying the possible linkages between individual cells.

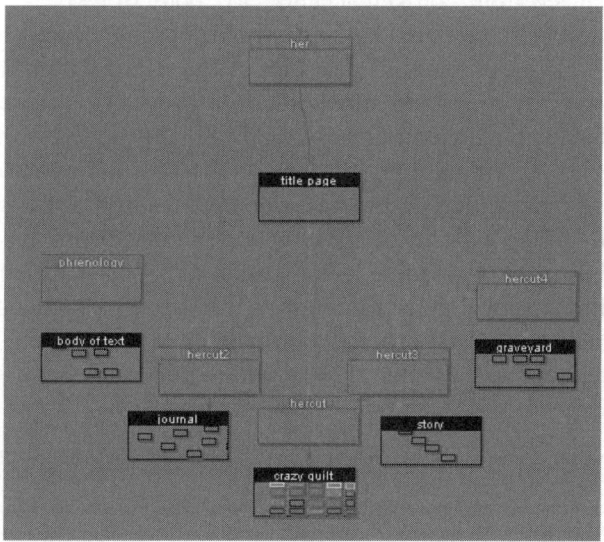

This visual presentation of the hypertext contrasts directly with its precursor form of the novel. A novel may possibly identify the titles of chapters and the page numbers on which they can be found in a table of contents, but there is no requirement for this and many novels that use

---

[4] The analogies between sewing and mapping, sewing and writing, and surgery and writing appear not only in Jackson's discussion of this work in "Stitch Bitch," but also in Hayles' article (paragraphs 33 and 39) and in Mark Amerika's interview of Jackson. In the "Reality Fiction" section of "Stitch Bitch," for instance, Jackson suggests that "by writing we test the seams, pick out the stitches, trying to stretch the gaps between things to slip out through them into some uncharted space."

[5] The map that appeals to me the most is the chart form, for it depicts the links clearly and identifies each page by title.

chapter divisions do not bother to display them in advance. The novel leaves the reader on a very practical level with scant indication of what to expect in what order and in what manner of narration.

The hypertext as Storyspace presents it, however, lays out the exact direction of the work, making it oddly difficult to deviate from the prescribed route.[6] Odd things happen here, though. The title page of the text indicates five chapters: "a graveyard, a journal, a quilt, a story & broken accents." The map, however, is at first confusing because it identifies the links to the chapter by titles of what turn out to be illustrations, but that link through to chapters that appear on the page in a different order than they had been on the title page.[7] These next links are also misleading not only because they are out of order, but because the first one, on the left, has had its name changed from "broken accents" to "body of text."[8]

Each chapter is represented by a box with miniscule boxes placed within it, each of which represents in turn one of the pages within that chapter. Clicking once on any of the smallest boxes opens it out so that its title appears. Double clicking on this box ought to make the page with text on it come into view.[9] Arrows from one box to the next indicate the links that Jackson has implemented to direct consecutive reading of the text pages.[10]

The ability of the hypertext to portray itself in map form sets up an interesting readjustment of reading as a spatial rather than a linear process. When reading a novel it is essential to proceed from one page to the next, in strictly sequential order. When reading this hypertext, even while Jackson often sets up the order of links within a chapter completely rigidly,

---

[6] How to explain my reluctance to click anywhere, as I could, but to follow the links in the order that they appear.

[7] These illustrations are the only pieces of the visual arts that Jackson included in this hypertext, a shame given the hypertext's essential need for a more complete integration of text and the visual forms. In fact, the text itself suffers from the continual gray of the background and the illegibility and blandness of the typeface. Granted, this hypertext was designed for individual use rather than for presentations, but when I projected it onto a screen for instructional purposes, my students experienced a great degree of difficulty in deciphering it.

[8] I am intrigued by my own response to this inconsistency. I have read plenty of hypertexts that provide no map whatsoever and feel perfectly comfortable with the literal disorientation that they can create. Perhaps it is just that in the face of possible clear sense of direction, I am irritated that it might not be perfect.

[9] Generally speaking, this would not occur for me, but it may be that I have been unable to find the page, for one of the vagaries of this program is that even when linking through from one text page to the next, the pages appear all over the place, often in corners from which they are difficult to extract. Once found, it takes several clicks to resize and center the window so that its contents are available for reading.

[10] I must express another reservation of the hypertext here because it fails to make fuller use of the randomness that could be set up in terms of one's passage through the text. Most pages include only one possible link to one other page, forcing readers to read sequentially and undermining the nonlinear approach of the hypertext genre to narration.

the order in which the chapters are read makes little to no difference to the reception of the work. While it is perhaps nice to know the origins of the girl's body parts before reading her "story," both the graveyard and story sections leave out critical background that each at least partially fulfills for each other.

The maps also prevent the disorientation immediately apparent in a succession of blind links that most hypertexts provide. The reader is always apprised of where he or she is in the hypertext at any particular moment and of the link selection available from each point in the space of the texts. The maps serve literally the function of maps in that they present the space of the text in such a way as to divide the space and orient it, to portion out its sections as if the hypertext were a physical landmass with geological features and compass points useful for finding bearings. "My reading," says the narrator in "this writing," "is spatial and even volumetric."

Crazy Quilt

There are two distinct types of narration in this hypertext, one of which is in traditional narrative form, "Story," a description of events in the Patchwork Girl's life told in sequence with, roughly, a beginning, a middle and an end and with, generally speaking, one link option per page so that it is only possible to read this section in a linear fashion. The rest of the segments of the hypertext, "Graveyard," "Journal," "Quilt," and "Broken Accents," embrace the more disruptive form of the hypertext, still often not permitting more than one link off of each page, but presenting the "story" of this Girl's creation and depiction in a nonlinear, non-sequential manner.

The "Quilt" is the section of this hypertext that appropriates materials from outside sources the most. In doing so, it replicates the composition of the Girl's body, as does the hypertext itself – a concatenation of ephemera drawn from a multitude of sources that bring into the new context of their use the continued attachment to their original derivation.[11] The "hidden figure" page of the "Story" section addresses this notion: "If all quotes [sic] remain tethered to their sources by however tenuous filaments, so my parts." An important aspect of appropriation is, however, the transformation of the quotation or body part in its new position, its new context, for what surrounds it is going to have an impact on its final nuance. The connection to the original source remains and influences its meaning, but the new context will change that meaning, will force the appropriated

---

[11] Jackson calls this hypertext a "collage of stories" ("Banished Body" in "Stitch Bitch").

material to adapt to the new situation. Even so, the continual reference to the previous existence of the quotations forces a discontinuous reading, a narration that fractures under the weight of voices from the past.

For me personally, the most resonant aspect of the appropriation comes from Mary Shelley's *Frankenstein*, for the vividness of her writing bursts through the blander style of Frank Baum and the theoretical discourse of the various critics and philosophers that Jackson incorporates into this text. In "scrap bag," for example, "profound study and laborious disquisition" take precedence for me over the other language. I see the pathetic Doctor Frankenstein desperately trying to save what little he has left in the world by putting together a female companion for the monster.

In "conception" the tremendous emotional cost of the doctor's labors surfaces in "I became nervous to a painful degree, the fall of a leaf startled me, and I shunned my fellow creatures as if I had been guilty of a crime." The rest of this page disrupts his pain, though, for it incorporates light references to the motley of a crazy quilt and, oddly, brings in an unrelated reference to writing and to the truth in remarks by Helene Cixous.

"beauty patches" is almost humorous in its juxtaposition of Shelley's words, "How delineate the wretch whom with such infinite pains and cares I had endeavored to form?" with a quotation from Klaus Theweleit's *Male Fantasies*: "A beautiful woman must have the voluptuous buttocks and lovely breasts of the ladies of England, the fiery glance of the women of Poland, a German body, and a podex from Paris." This is a humor, though, that fissures the flow of the narrative, by focusing our attention to the distance between the serious fervor of the scientist and the sexual proclivities of a philanderer.

This disjunctive quality is perhaps at its height on the "labor" page where the monster is brought to life. The quotation from Shelley is one of the more memorable in the novel: "My candle was nearly burnt out, when, by the glimmer of the half-extinguished light, I saw the dull yellow eye of the creature open; it breathed hard, and a convulsive motion agitated its limbs." That "dull yellow eye" will remain with me forever and always call to mind the endless rain and stormy weather and chill of that moody Romantic novel. It doesn't "go" smoothly with the rest of this page, the Glass Cat and Magician of Baum's *The Patchwork Girl of Oz*, or the "proper woman" of Cixous. I admit that this reading is heavily influenced by my knowledge of Shelley's novel, but isn't this the point here, that it is impossible to sever completely a quotation from its original source?

The appropriation works particularly well, however, when Jackson turns to the ridiculous portion of *Frankenstein* where the monster learns to read and write and understand language almost as if by osmosis in "write?"

Here the monster's discovery of someone's portmanteau lost on the road is followed by Cixous' equally ridiculous description of the importance of books to her: "The possession of these treasures gave me extreme delight. I beat my books; I caressed them. Page after page, O beloved, licked, lacerated." Following these completely absurd passages is a section of nonsense verse from Baum that emphasizes their preposterousness. Even so, by forcing attention to the inanity of these sections and to comparisons between them, the text heightens awareness of the disjunctiveness of appropriation.

Fleshly Voyage

In the "typographical" section of "Story" the narrator identifies one of the main purposes of this hypertext, to relate a "body" of writing to the human body: "The comparison between a literary composition and the fitting together of the human body from various members stemmed from ancient rhetoric." The idea that this comparison has been made since the time of Plato establishes the extent to which western culture accepts it.[12] The text continues here by relating various examples of writing as related to the physical body, for this is what this hypertext endeavors to do, to create the girl's body and by extension her identity by piecing together textual components that at the same time create the physical but more conceptual entity of the text itself.[13]

Jackson goes beyond this effort, in fact, by suggesting that writing itself determines bodies, that human existence but especially the existence of women is predicated on the act of writing about individuals, about one's own self. "You could say that all bodies are written bodies, all lives pieces of writing" confirms this point in "all written." This statement is a clear reference to the theories of Julia Kristeva and Helene Cixous, the latter of whom is one of the sources for this hypertext. Kristeva's *sujet en proces* and Cixious' writing through the body in the act of bringing the woman's body into existence are, in fact, critical components of the theories driving Jackson's work.[14]

---

[12] Hayles uses the body as a metaphor for this hypertext, too, referring to it as a "'body of text'" (paragraph 23), and saying that "like the female monster's body, the body of this hypertext is also seemed and ruptured, comprised of disparate parts with extensive links between them" (paragraph 23).
[13] "Like the body," Jackson suggests in the "Everything at Once" section of "Stitch Bitch," hypertext "has no point to make, only clusters of intensities, and one cluster is as central as another."
[14] See Helene Cixous, "The Laugh of the Medusa," Signs 1 (1976): 875-93, and Julia Kristeva, La Revolution du poetique. L'avant-garde a la fin du XIXe siecle: Lautreamont et Mallarme,

In a sense, Jackson's direct address of the act of creating this hypertext sets up an internal and relatively more conceptual map of the hypertext itself. "Assembling these patched words in an electronic space" from "this writing" calls attention to Jackson's need to take pieces of text and link them together just as the quilt is a map of stitched scraps and the girl is a body of sutured fragments.

By seeing identity as fragmentary, too, Jackson had to create a new fictional form to mirror the broken slivers of identity. In "I made myself over," she explains this: "I began to invent something new: a way to hang together without pretending I was whole." To make over is to redo with the understanding that what is already there is inadequate or inaccurate. To hang together is not only an expression of the adherence of disparate parts, to spend time together, but also to exist in a state of alliance with one another, to concur, to support.[15] These parts of identity can only provide ease of being through the ability to see them differently and to see them in a manner that permits consensus.

This text portrays the recasting of identity as a maternal art, but as an endeavor that is perhaps misguided and as mistaken as the creator of the monster. "Through art," says the narrator in "misconception," "one could even breed misfits and transform them into a new species. 'Mosaic' technique of the maternal imagination, mistress of errors; aren't you the very demon of multiplicity?" This passage seems, indeed, quite disjunctive in a text devoted to the creation of a unified being from the scattered shards of personality components; it reinforces, in fact, the splintered nature of the products of artistic endeavor.

The narrator (and should I be saying "Jackson" here?) talks to us directly about how she makes this text, though, and how this text is like the quilt, that emblem of the girl's body and subjectivity.[16] In "a single space" she says, "I cut up the quilt, creating a new copy of each paragraph in its

---

Paris: Edition du Seuil, 1974, 316. Mary Ann Doane points out some of the risks involved in feminist focus on the female body in "The Voice in the Cinema: The Articulation of Body and Space": "A political erotics which posits a new phantasmatic, which relies on images of an 'extended' sensory body, is inevitably caught in the double bind which feminism always seem to confront: on the one hand, there is a danger in grounding a politics on a conception of the body because the body has always been *the* site of a woman's oppression posted as the final and undeniable guarantee of a difference and a lack; bout on the other hand, there is a potential gain as well – it is precisely because the body has been a major site of oppression that perhaps it must be the site of the battle to be waged. The supreme achievement of patriarchal ideology is that it has no outside" (374).

[15] As Jackson says in the "Constellation" section of "Stitch Bitch": "I am a loose aggregate.... But hypertext provides a body."

[16] The quilt has been a forceful symbol of female identity in feminist theory, since and probably before Adrienne Rich's attention to it in "Transcendental Etude." As Kathleen Fraser said to me not so long ago, "Women's lives are fragmentary, and their work reflects this multiplicity."

own writing space." Clearly, she recreated what was a unified and linear text in the new and disjunctive environment of the hypertext in her effort to depict identity as it really is. In "composition" she says, "You organize writing spaces by grouping them together on the screen, and by placing writing spaces inside other spaces, and one thing so presupposes another that whichever way you turn your patchwork, the figures still seem ill-arranged." The impact of splitting up the writing into separate pages and permitting a resorting of the order of access to them is to break up a sense of unified identity, but to allow a more accurate rendering of subjectivity in its irrevocably fractured constantly shifting and flickering state.

The graveyard is the place to start this voyage through the body, as it provides the material for the girl's body, a form composed of pieces of corpses scavenged from a variety of graves. The first page of the graveyard depicts this source literally, the title page's image of the girl cut up and rearranged, each piece surrounded by dotted lines so that the segments can be cut apart and sorted to reassemble her portrayal.[17] A fragment of text in the upper corner confirms the task here: "You may continue to flesh out this planning study." The play on words of "flesh" is telling as it's one of those interesting words in English that is its own antonym. To flesh out

---

[17] Hayles discusses the dotted line at length in "Flickering Connectiveness" in terms of its ability to "separate and connect" but also in terms of its "suggestions that the image can move from two to three dimensions, as in a fold-up..." (paragraphs 25-6).

means to add material or to gain weight, but in its transitive form the verb refers to the stripping of flesh from the skeleton, to create an appetite in hunting animals like dogs or falcons for the taste of flesh, to accustom one to bloodshed, to thrust a weapon into flesh as well as to fill out, to delineate. The process of creating the girl by linking through from piece to piece of her composition is at the same time the act of stripping her of her body, limb by limb, identity by identity.

The first page of text, the only one linked to the title page of this "chapter," directs the reader to put the girl together by sewing her together "piecemeal." Again, as with flesh, piecemeal refers to a bit-by-bit process, that the girl's body must be fastened together limb by limb and organ by organ, but also that an entity is in pieces, it can only be seen in terms of its parts and not as a coherent whole. The tone here is one of admonishment – the work is up to the reader.[18]

The only link available connects to the "headstone," not an image of one, but in typography perhaps suggesting one, and certainly in the linguistic structure of one:

> Here lies a Head, Trunk, Arms (Right and Left), and Legs
> (Right and Left)
> as well as Divers Organs Appropriately Disposed.
> May They Rest in Piece.

The joke here is obvious. A headstone is meant to identify the person lying dead under it by name. Instead the text provides a list of body parts, removing demarcating features of gender and identity. Again, too, the suggestion that the body parts "rest in piece" indicates the uselessness of the effort to put them together in its pun on the peaceful rest in eternity – this rest is disrupted.

Each part listed on the headstone has a direct link to a body part. I have started with the head: "My skull is like an ancient vase" the fragments of which have been dug up and glued together by archaeologists. The relation of the body to clay is not a new idea. In Genesis, for instance, God takes up "dust of the ground" to make man.[19] Also, it is intriguing that the writer chose "vase" for this metaphor. "Urn" would have more funereal implications; vessel perhaps more biological. "Vase" is elite and decorative and therefore less useful. What is important about this skull is that the pieces of ceramic that have been fastened together may or may not come from the same vase, multiplying the sources of its final shape. The narrator says,

---

[18] Joyce emphasizes this effort on the part of the reader when he says that "hypertext... implicates the reader in writing" (580).
[19] A striking example of clay formed into the body appears in Edward FitzGerald's *The Rubaiyat of Omar Khayyam*.

"Sometimes when it's quiet I hear in my ears the roaring of a crowd." Each shard of clay brings its own voice to bear in the creation of the cranial cavity.

The only link from the head is the eyeballs, organs taken from the body of a handicapped woman, Tituba, who, confined to her room, read a great deal and could see the goings on in the village beneath her window. While the narrator claims that these eyes provide a "clear and sharp" vision and a "gaze calm and speculative," their goodness is undermined by Tituba's publishing a chronicle of scandalous events in the village. It is important to note here that the character of the original owner transmits itself through her most valuable physical asset.

The girl's lips come from Margaret who laughed freely all her life, in spite of her hardships. Her tongue comes from Susannah, "who talked more than she ate and ate more than the baker and butcher combined." Her ears have been harvested from Flora. They are "large, slightly furred, saucer shaped, and almost ornate with cartilaginous flourishes." Flora listens to everything and learns all that she can about everyone, but she, unlike Susannah and Tituba, keeps her secrets.

This tension between the Patchwork Girl's body parts is irresolvable. For while the parts have been sewn together to create her body, they are continually at war with one another. The Girl may hear everything and may see everything, but her ears admonish her to be discrete and her eyes seek revenge on the world for Tituba's physical impairments.

The most telling example of this internal conflict is literally internal: in the Girl's bowels, what the text refers to as "Guts," a word with visceral and animal connotations. The upper portion of the Girl's intestines was taken from Mistress Anne, a woman of great organization and efficiency, who "[evacuated] her bowels with exemplary thoroughness." The Girl has a relatively large-scale physique, however, so Mistress Anne's intestines were not long enough to extend between stomach and anus, and the lower portion of the colon of a cow was grafted in to bridge the gap. The problem is that the upper portion of the Girl's intestines is very moderate and regular, but the lower portion takes its time to come to the decision to defecate, and when it does so, it evacuates quite suddenly and explosively and explosively, inducing great embarrassment in the Mistress Anne section. The pieces of the Girl's body that have been incorporated into her therefore retain the character of the original owner so that the differing impulses of these segments clash and vitiate the adjoining seams' efforts to make the Girl's identity coalesce.

Another clear example of this internal struggle is the girl's right arm. The upper part of it came from the corpse of a woman, Tristessa, who scorned men and dogs and never hesitated to throw missiles at them with unfailingly accurate aim. The lower section of the right arm came from a delicate society woman, Eleanor, who "wielded a fan like a weapon, unfurling and snapping it shut with militant flirtatiousness," using social female skills to manipulate her surroundings. Either way, each part of the arm is to be regarded with caution, as the Girl says: "One part of me hurls weapons for a welcome. One part uses welcome as a weapon. On one thing they agree: when I look friendly, take care." Again, the irreconcilable battle between overt physical threat and relatively more subversive social control renders the Girl incapable of action and places her in a never-ending whirl of indecision.

Even so, the point here is whether or not *Patchwork Girl* depicts character as accurately as is possible in the abstract environment of fiction and of fiction-related media, and based on Deleuze and Guattari's model of subjectivity (indicated as one of Jackson's sources), this hypertext may in fact provide an acceptable rendering of the Girl. It enables, in fact, according to Deleuze and Guattari, the representation of the focus of manifold threads of meaning that bind together to form individual identity. In their 1973 essay, "May 14, 1914. One or Several Wolves?" they suggest: "The proper name does not designate an individual: it is on the contrary when the individual opens up to the multiplicities pervading him or her, at the outcome of the most severe operation of depersonalization that he or she acquires his or her true proper name. The proper name is the subject of a pure infinitive comprehended as such in a field of intensity" (146). By denying the Girl a proper name, in essence, Jackson establishes her very being by permitting the separate strands of the variable components of her body to create who she is in the absence of the rigid calcification of the name.[20]

In such a manner in the "story" section of the hypertext the Girl takes on someone else's name, Elsie. When the girl falls apart, Elsie says in "name," "You'll have to find another, because I'm taking mine back."[21] It is once the Girl gives up Elsie's name that she comes to some sense of identity, an identity composed of these disparate elements that may in fact depict as accurate a sense of character as anything, a multiple composite identity.[22]

Jackson incorporates a quotation by Deleuze and Guattari into the "many brains" page that confirms subjectivity as more an amalgam than a coherent unified mass: "And if we imagined the position of a fascinated

---

[20] Jackson points out in "We Like to Make Statues" and "Everything at Once" in "Stitch Bitch" that "desire rather than identity is [hypertext's] compositional principle."
[21] Jackson refers to the changeable features of the body and of identity in the "Banished Body" section of "Stitch Bitch" by calling the body "simultaneous," and "unstable."
[22] Again, this is a reference, I believe, to Kristeva's *sujet en proces*. Hayles also identifies the monster's body as "multiple" and "fragmented" (paragraph 27).

Self, it was because the multiplicity towards which it leans... is the continuation of another multiplicity that works it and strains it from the inside." This sense of the manifold nature of identity recurs in this hypertext in all senses – the girl's body, the hypertext itself, the disjunctive narration – but most explicitly in "identities" and "bodies too" where the narrator suggests that "we are coupled to constructions of meaning; we are legible, partially; we are cooperative with meanings, but irreducible to any one."[23] The use of the first person plural here is embracing, including not only the patchwork girl, her creator, her writer, her hypertextual environment, but us, the readers and all human beings. Much of this statement is clearly poststructuralist (identity as constructed), but much of it is also allied with theories of human existence as heterogeneous in nature, as reflective of individual experiences and components that assemble within one body, all the parts of which continuing to yell about their other contexts, their other states of being in the same way that the patchwork girl's physical parts retain allegiances to their first owner[24].

Works Cited

Amerika, Mark. "Stitch Bitch: The Hypertext Author As Cyborg-Femme Narrator." Telepolis (March 3, 1998). accessed 7/10/00. http://www.heise.de/tp/english/inhalt/kolu/3193/1.html

Buschert, William and Nebojsa Kujundzic. "The Closure of Imagination: The Poetics of Virtual Reality and the Body." Canadian Review of Comparative Literature 24.2 (June 1997): 211-17.

Cixous, Helene. "The Laugh of the Medusa." Signs 1 (1976): 875-93.

Deleuze, Gilles, and Felix Guattari. "May 14, 1914: One or Several Wolves?" Semiotext(e) 2.3 (1973): 137-47.

Doane, Mary Ann. "The Voice in the Cinema: The Articulation of body and Space." 363-375 in Film Theory and Criticism: Introductory Readings. Leo Braudy and Marshall Cohens, Eds. Oxford: Oxford University Press, 1999.

Hayles, N. Katharine. "Flickering Connectivities in Shelley Jackson's Patchwork Girl: The Importance of Media-Specific Analysis," *Postmodern Culture* 10.2 (2000). accessed 7/10/00. http://www.iath.virginia.edu/pmc/text-only/issue.100/10.2hayles.txt

---

[23] Meira Weiss argues that "we are the narrators of our bodies, that bodies can ba chosen by each of us from a myriad or cultural-collective representations, and that this narration, like any oral narration, is regulated by society" (255). This approach also calls to mind the phenomenology of such theorists as Sartre and Merleau-Ponty who contend that the body is in an endless reciprocity with experience and actions, being formed by them as much as acting upon them. See, too, William Buschert and Nebojsa Kujundzic's "The Closure of Imagination," 212.

[24] An interesting example of this attitude towards identity is the character of Sally in Tim Burton's *A Nightmare Before Christmas* in which she takes apart her body to use the parts for separate purposes, to vamp the monster, to save Santa Claus, to escape captivity.

Jackson, Shelley. *Patchwork Girl*. Watertown, MA: Eastgate Systems, 1996.
— "Stitch Bitch: The patchwork girl." text of Jackson's presentation at the Transformations of the Book Conference, MIT, October 24-25, 1998. accessed 7/10/00. URL: http://media-in-transition.mit.edu/articles/jackson.html
Joyce, Michael. "Nonce Upon Some Times: Rereading Hypertext Fiction" *Modern Fiction Studies* 43.3 (Fall 1997): 579-597.
Kristeva, Julia. *La Revolution du poetique. L'avant-garde a la fin du XIXe siecle: Lautreamont et Mallarme*, Paris: Edition du Seuil, 1974.
Merleau-Ponty, Maurice. *Phenomenology of Perception*. London: Routledge and Kegan Paul, 1962.
Sartre, Jean-Paul. *The Psychology of Imagination*. New York: Citadel, 1948.
Weiss, Meira. "Narratives of Embodiment: The discursive formulation of multiple bodies." *Semiotica* 118.3-4 (1998): 239-60.

In Search of *Califia*

Raine Koskimaa
(IT University of Copenhagen)

M. D. Coverley (pen name for Marjorie Luesebrink) has written several relatively small scale Web fictions (*Endless Suburbs, Life in the Chocolate Mountains, Fibonacci's Daughter* etc.), poetry (*RainFrames*), parts of various Web collaborations ("Elys, The Lacemaker" from *The Book of Hours of Madame de Lafayette*) – and the strongly multimedial hypernovel *Califia* (2000). Luesebrink has also been an active participant in the ongoing discussions about the possibilities of digital and networked writing. Her paper in the Ninth ACM Conference on Hypertext and Hypermedia, "The Moment in Hypertext: A Brief Lexicon of Time," was an important opening for the discussion of temporality in hypertext (Luesebrink 1998).

Califia is a manifold story about seeking a lost treasure somewhere in California (Califia being the name of that treasure). It is a story of three families and five generations – needless to say, the families are complexly intertwined. On one level, *Califia* tells about three friends, Augusta Summerland, Kaye Beveridge and Calvin, who are all interested in the gold treasure known as a family myth both in Summerland's and Beveridge's families. The stories of four previous generations – of a treasure gained, hidden, found, hidden again, and eventually lost; of romances, financial deals and betrayals; of crimes – are as much of interest as the treasure proper. The surface level consists of four journeys that Augusta, Kaye and Calvin take in order to explore that history.

In addition to the surface level narrative there is a wealth of other materials: historical narratives told in chronological order, myths and legends related to the stories, and diverse documents: from newspaper clippings to receipts, to deeds, to journal entries, to maps, etc. The surface level quickly turns to a frame story for the unfolding historical narratives (or a narrative, since it all connects to a more or less coherent history). This as an eternal treasure hunt, in which the reader is invited to participate. The reader may find her own trail through the wealth of information and stories gathered in one form or another – but the story also escapes the boundaries of fiction, into reality, as far as one can speak of reality in California (cf. Baudrillard); true to the spirit of historiographic metafiction, there is so much documentary and quasi-documentary material included that the reader is tempted to go to the Los Angeles Public Library, as recommended in the text, and look for even more information from the newspapers and other documents held there. It is also claimed, in the preface to the third part of *Califia*, that some of the documents described there were sent to Augusta, Kaye and Calvin by readers interested in the whereabouts of the treasure. Also, in the end the reader is urged to submit her own experiences in the treasure seeking to Kaye, Augusta and Calvin.

The Raiders of the Lost Califia

On one level *Califia* is a quest and a mystery while it also has its share of romance. Augusta Summerland's father dies and soon after, a Wind Power Company offers to buy a worthless piece of land her father owned. Just when Augusta is ready to sign a contract, she meets Kaye Beveridge, who begs her not to. She introduces herself and quite soon Augusta is convinced (if not convinced, at least interested in the claim) that the piece of land has something to do with a gold treasure known in both the Summerland and the Beveridge family. Augusta's father believed in the treasure, and tried to locate it, even though he has not committed his whole life to this task, as many others have. Augusta did not give the gold too much thought, but now Kaye makes her interested in the stories. Augusta's neighbor, Calvin, is also drawn into the quest. He knows Augusta's family quite well (and he has also heard stories about some treasure) – but the connection between Calvin and Kaye is rather vague. It is Kaye, after all, who invites Calvin to join them; he is more than happy to do so.

They will take several trips, mostly all three together, to the Paradise Home where Augusta's mother is being treated care for her Alzheimer's Disease, to meet the Wind Power representatives, to meet Augusta's aunt Rosalind (whose whereabouts Augusta learns only after her father's death), and to the Los Angeles Harbor. During these trips, through discussions with various people they meet, a wealth of stories about their ancestors, and of Califia, is revealed – maybe the most important piece of news, told by Aunt Rosalind, is that Calvin's real name is Calvino Lugo (he has been raised in foster families); his real parents were Tibby Lugo and Nellie Clare Beveridge, which makes him the second cousin of Kaye, and also, as integral a part of the Califia story as Augusta and Kaye are. Between the trips,

Augusta, Kaye and Calvin consult the documents Augusta's father left behind; and Kaye consults the spirits...

Alongside Augusta's chronological narrative there are Kaye's mythologies and legends, as well as documentary material archived by Calvin. These may be read in any order – there are paths through each of the sections (Augusta's path, Kaye's path, Calvin's path), but there are numerous text links between the paths, and, additionally, there are several navigational devices with which the materials can be read (making a digression to some sub-plot; consulting maps, looking through collected contracts and business letters, opening a new window for watching photographs etc.) In *Califia*, the hypertext structure is not used to create alternative storylines, but as an archive from which different aspects of the main story can be sought.

> Our memories are always in the process of revision. As Kaye is quick to point out, a composite version of the same event is as close as we might come to truth. Even so, the contour of reality is as elusive as the Terrestrial Paradise. ("To the Reader, Part III")

The materials belong to three different temporal levels: the present time (the textual actual world), the historical time (as recounted in stories, and recorded in documents), and the mythical time (the time of astrology and North American Indian mythology). The three main characters each focus on one of these levels, which produces somewhat differing alternatives:

> Dear Fellow Prospector:
>
> You may find the rhythm of the story and the cadence of the steps enough. Or you may wish to understand the structure of our project. Because it is three-dimensional, and because it is evolving, Augusta, Kaye, and I see the outline differently... ("Topological Maps")

From Interface Time to Mythical Time

Time and space are two fundamental categories with which we structure the world around us. As spatiality has been extensively discussed in theory and to some extent exploited in practice, it seems odd that temporal issues have been on a sidetrack in the hypertext discussion so far.[1] One exception has been Luesebrink's presentation at the *Hypertext 98* conference about time in hyperfiction. She makes a basic distinction between "Interface time" and "Cognitive time," the former describing the real time activities when reading hyperfiction, the latter describing the time related to the fictional

---

[1] However, Espen Aarseth's theory of cybertextuality (1997) has established a new frame in which to discuss temporal issues; see especially Eskelinen (1998 and 2001).

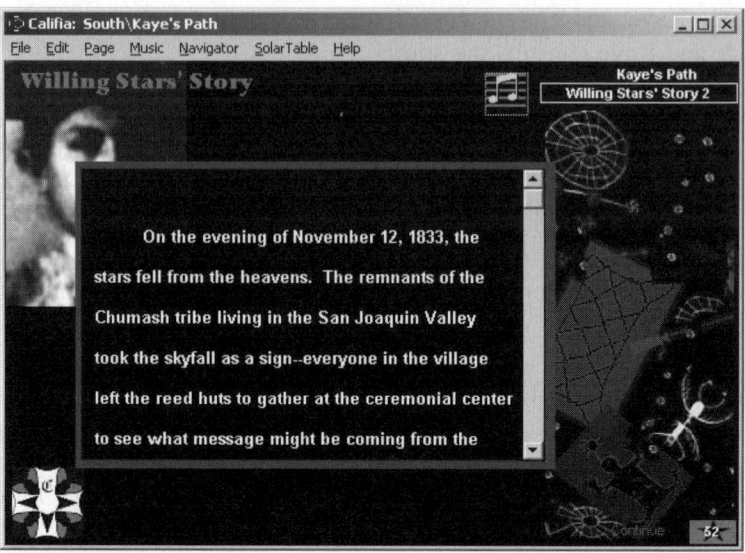

world. Each of these categories is further divided into three different modes (Luesebrink 1998: 107-111):

Interface time: mechanical (time spent waiting for the program to load etc.), reading (the actual time spent reading the text), interactive (the time spent in interaction with the text – navigation etc.)

Cognitive: real (time of the narration), narrative (time of the narrated, historical time), mythic (the cyclical time of mythologies)

The category of interface time is fine as such, and its internal distinctions are necessary and useful. Cognitive time is also a useful concept, although I may be giving it a somewhat different meaning than Luesebrink does in her definition. As real time I understand the time of narration or the time of the fictional actual world (thus, real time in the fictive world), narrative time is the time of the narrator (fictional history). Mythic time is a concept which functions as a leak between ontological boundaries – it is something shared between the actual world and the worlds of fiction, a zone that is not possible to attribute to either one of them.[2] The numerous references to actual history and actual historical figures (like the actress Bette Davis) in *Califia* serve to give the text an authentic, documentary feeling – these references can be explained, depending on the theoretical framework, either as referring to the reality outside the fictional sphere, or, as referring to fictional objects (historical figures being "fictionalized" in the text).

---

[2] This comes close to Thomas G. Pavel's (1986) idea of different ontological spheres of which the borders are constantly in flux.

Mythology, on the other hand, is something not real (in the positivist sense), it could be compared to abstract categories like mathematical axioms; it is not realistic, or fictional, but mythical, and thus transcending the limits of the fictional world (Harshaw 1984).

In *Califia*, then, real and historical time are clearly separated, whereas the mythical time is always present (see Figure below). Real time is open, in a constant process of becoming, historical time is linear, and mythic time is cyclical. In *Califia* this is closely related to all the cyclical phenomena in nature, especially to celestial movements. Star charts – the Big Dipper, Ursa Major – play a central role in the efforts to locate the treasure.

Historical time plays the role of the adversary here; it corrodes memory, and ruins the landmarks: "The past is fractured and changed and forgotten" ("Ernie's Skull"). Mythical time offers the eternal, although enigmatic, directions. In *Califia*, the time and space *chronotope* plays a crucial role. All three temporal levels are simultaneously present, inscribed in the geological and cultural landscape (see figures above and below).

The category of cognitive time is not specific to hypertext fiction – we can detect the three levels of cognitive time in most fictions. Hypertext, however, and especially hypermedia, seems exceptionally well suited for presenting mythic time. Through hyperlinks and the hypertextual structure, the elements of mythic time can be distributed all over the work; mythic time in a very concrete way permeates the whole of the Califia story.

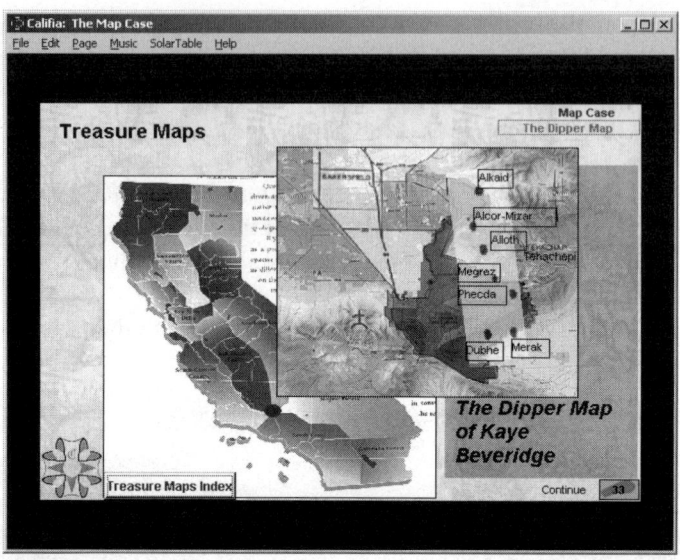

The Virtual Space of Califia

Spatiality has always been one of the central topics in discussions about hypertext, but spatial presentation has been used sparsely in actual hypertext novels. Works like Shelley Jackson's *Patchwork Girl* (1995), and Deena Larsen's *Samplers. Nine Vicious Little Hypertexts* (1997) use the spatial map as a site for signification, but in a very schematic way. The possibilities hinted at as well as some features borrowed from computer games, are used in a highly original way in *Califia*. In *Califia* there are several ways for navigation: star charts, geological maps, timelines etc., all of which structure the text in their own way. Each of the three main characters are also focalizers for different approaches to the story/stories, and offer different ways to approach the totality of the materials in *Califia* (Augusta focusing on the chronological order of real time events, Calvin on the arranging of historical materials, and Kaye on the mythological and ancient stories).

The text is furnished with a wealth of images – both pictures and symbolic images – which often function simultaneously as illustrations and navigating devices. There is the basic Windows menu bar at the top of the screen, but the rest of the screen is reserved for content, which also serves the function of navigation. Instead of providing a cognitive map of the hypertextual structure, the reader is confronted with geographical maps (often juxtaposed with star charts and treasure maps), which situate the historical and real time events spatially. In other words, pictures showing the locations give a local spatiality for the events.

This is a very different approach from the spatialization of hypertext as employed in the "classical hypertexts." Instead of relying solely on the spatial aspect of the hypertextual structure, the fictional world is represented as a proto-virtual reality which depicts the hypertextual structure and sub-structures in a naturalized way. This is a good example of the integration of navigation devices into the (hyper)fictional world.

Califia presents us with an interactive environment into which the reader can – as with many computer games – get him/herself immersed. A good case for comparison is the Broderbund game *Myst* by Rand and Robyn Miller. In *Myst* the reader/player can enter the closed world of an island and wander around, solving numerous problems and fulfilling different tasks. It is as close to the immersive virtual reality experience as it is possible to get without Virtual Reality devices like data helmets. At the same time, however, it has a strong textual element: there are several (partly decayed) books and notes on the island, which are crucial for problem solving. But these texts in *Myst* have another, possibly an even more important function: they provide a narrative for the otherwise "narrativeless" world. The passages in the books are related to different instruments on the island, and in some way they can be said to be hypertextually linked to each other (although the links are not immediate or even obvious); thus, one could argue that *Myst* is a hypertext narrative with an elaborate 3D reader interface...

When placed side by side, *Califia* and *Myst* show us the difference between hyperfiction and virtual reality. Even though the text fragments have an important role in *Myst*, they are still functioning as one subcategory of effects in that game, and no conclusion can be drawn that text would somehow be necessary in all virtual realities aiming at delivering a narrative.[3] In *Califia*, on the other hand, everything is language, albeit in many instances symbolic language. In Jay David Bolter's terms, everything in *Califia* is simultaneously meant to be looked through (creating the fictional world) and looked at (functioning as a metatextual device), while in Virtual Reality (as in *Myst*) everything is meant to be looked through (Bolter 1996).

Language has a capacity for creating worlds often attributed to its indetermination, openness or even vagueness: language evokes a world but leaves it open for the human imagination to complete it in a proper way. Illustrations,

---

[3] Søren Pold has written about the "scripted space" in games like *Myst*, arguing that each of the screens in *Myst* are "scripted" to contain fragments of stories (Pold 1998).

dramatizations and filmatizations of texts always encounter the criticism that they tie the receivers' imagination to a prefabricated model, thus weakening much of the representational power of the original text. One of the central techniques in *Califia*, to avoid restricting the imagination this way, is its use of symbolic language – from astrology and Indian mythology to geographical maps etc. – which provide illustrations that are powerful as pictures, but because of their symbolic nature do not have the restrictive effect realistic illustrations would have. Because of this advantage, it is not surprising to notice that *Samplers* is also based on symbolic representation (drawn also from North American Indian mythology) – as is Adrianne Wortzel's Web fiction *Electronic Chronicles* (1995). Maps are of course one of the more obvious choices for navigating, mainly because they are made for that purpose in the first place, but also because they are easily motivated in the fictional world. *Califia*, however, makes the solution more interesting in juxtaposing several maps, motivating the hypertextual structure through the limitless variations of juxtaposing these maps.

The juxtaposing of several different, and even incompatible, spaces produces a *heterotopic space*, as Michel Foucault has termed it in his article "Of Other Spaces" (1986). A typical heterotopia is a cathedral, where sacred and profane spaces are juxtaposed. According to Foucault, the sacred spaces are quickly vanishing from our culture – because of that, we badly need new ways to experience the immersion in the sacred. I have argued elsewhere that the virtual spaces of cyberpunk science fiction, alongside other functions, work as heterotopic sites, where the sacred finds a realm for a return (think about the voodoo deities in the Matrix of William Gibson's *Neuromancer*, or the mystic qualities of The Other Plane in Vernor Vinge's "True Names," and the virtual realities in Pat Cadigan's *Synners*).[4] The hypertextual, virtual space of Califia the project works in the same way, bringing the mythological principles to the same level as the other means of structuring the stories and the data related to them (at one point Kaye does mention the similarity between the structure of *Califia* and that of the *Kabbalah*). In this it echoes the feelings of JackRabbit Jack, one of the earlier hunters:

> He wanted to protect the fragments of meaning that kept slipping away from him. Create a bastion against a future that would hold no promise of magic ("Fish Camp Factfinding").

The other spaces (as Foucault calls them), are also spaces for the Other.

---

[4] Koskimaa 1997b; see also McClure (1995) about spirituality in postmodernist fiction, and Davis (1993).

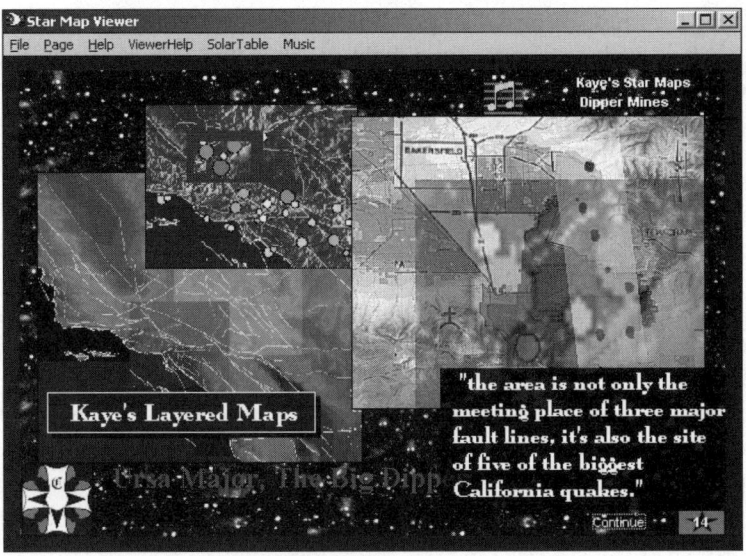

The Eternal Circle of Interpretation

Augusta, arguably the protagonist of *Califia*, narrates the quest in chronological order. This way a general understanding of the Califia history of the three families is formed, as the three main persons combine their knowledge of family stories and myths, and integrate the information they receive from other persons. While following "Augusta's Path" through the text, this is the picture the reader gets – a very general overview of the main characters and events for over 150 years and five generations. Augusta's mother's eventual death, as well as Kaye's and Calvin's relationship growing intimate, are recounted in the chronological story.

Calvin's role in the quest is to keep the information in order. He arranges the documents Augusta's father left behind in an archive; he provides them (and the reader too) with a map case, including everything from route maps to maps concerning different geological features of the California landscape (fault lines, land slides, earthquake sites etc.); there is a photo album etc. And it is Calvin who types in the story (written by Augusta) on computer. *Califia* – the work we are reading – is assumedly the electronic document Calvin has built for them to help keep the mass of documents and information in order. This way we readers are in a sense put in an equal position to the fictional characters as users of the very same archival program.

All the documents in the archives (theoretically, in all existing archives holding documents in some way relevant to the history of the last two hundred years in California; in practice, all the documents held in Calvin's archive) help us better understand, help us fill in the gaps in the stories told in the Summerland and Beveridge families. As such, these documents are only of limited interest; only when we know something about the events they are related to, they start making sense to us.

> As for documents in the study, they tell the story in the way ancient history reveals itself – fragmented and motive-free. A narrative of indirection ("JackRabbitt Jack 3").

This is the basic situation when we are dealing with attempts to understand, or interpret, all kinds of phenomena. There must be some kind of pre-understanding on which the larger picture is based, and after that there is circular movement between the general understanding and details. Each new bit of information, its significance, is first, provisionally, interpreted from the viewpoint of the whole – while it also has the potential to change the whole picture, and to change the previous interpretations of other information.

> Rosalind seems to be rather good at arranging narratives to hide secrets. So expert, perhaps, that she has buried whole episodes in cold storage, in packages without names. Secret keeping is one way of coping with realities (...). "That part of the story exists in different versions in my mind," she says slowly. "One version is what I believed at the time and continued to consider as the official family account. Another has all the later revelations, the elements that fill in the spaces, answering questions we didn't want to ask" ("North Point 4").

The family myths and legends the three characters share with each other – and, through Augusta's chronological story, with the readers – function as the pre-understanding for *Califia*. The "docudramas" Calvin and Kaye construct serve as a "first round" for the circle of interpretation. They are short stories, depicting certain episodes in the Califia history, centered on one person or another. They are assumedly based on known facts of those persons' lives and filled in with guess work by Kaye and Calvin – the stories imagined in such a way that they fit both the big picture and the given details. These mininarratives, in their turn, help us get a clearer understanding of the whole.

New findings along the way help us to fill in particular gaps in the stories, or direct us to make minor adjustments to the big picture. There are bigger revelations, though, one of them being Aunt Rosalind's story about Calvin's, or, Calvino's, childhood. We learn, first, that Calvin is really Calvino Lugo, which is significant, since the Lugos play almost as big a role in the Califia history as the Summerlands and the Beveridges. Additionally, we learn that his mother was Nelly Clare Beveridge, which fills in a big gap in both Nelly Clare's and Tibby Lugo's stories – before

Aunt Rosalind's story Nelly Clare disappeared in 1939. Now we know that she ended up in the La Liebre with Tibby, and lived there at least long enough to give birth to Calvin.

This kind of hermeneutic activity, and especially its explicit thematization in the story, is common to all mystery stories. What is different in *Califia* is its open ending – or better yet – its non-closure. There is no final answer – it may be that Augusta and her friends have located the treasure, but there have been several predecessors who have also believed this, only to be let down time after time. To prove that they have finally found the right place would require a massive excavation in the mountains – an effort possibly too expensive and risky for them to ever undertake. The 'answer' or definite ending for the quest, is not sought after at all; what is more important is the process itself, knowledge of the place and its inhabitants gained during the search. *Califia*, then, turns to a metaphysical quest rather than a conventional mystery. While metaphysical quests, almost by definition, tend to be universal in nature, there is in *Califia* a very strong sense of place – firmly grounded in the geography and history of California. While the eternal quest as such is universal, this particular quest for Califia could not take place anywhere else than in California – as is said somewhere in the text: "The place matters."

The circular movement is also mirrored in the narrative structure of *Califia*. The story is told in four parts, each recording one round trip returning to the starting point, Augusta's house. In the transitory phases between the trips, there is reflection, interpretation, and conclusion, before a new round trip. The four parts are titled according to the general direction of the trip: "South: The Comets in the Yard," "North: Night of the Bear," "East: Wind, Sand, and Stars," and finally, "West: The Journey Out." The West, and the Pacific Ocean, offer a possibility to step out of the endless cycle, a step necessarily metaphysical in nature – as wonderfully illustrated by Violet's (Augusta's recently died mother) spirit walking to the Pacific surf. In another form, there is the possibility to exit the fictional world. For those, who are not yet taking that step, the cycle continues.

This openendedness can be seen in connection to the proto-virtual reality-like quality of *Califia*. It is at least as much a landscape to wander in and out, as a narrative with a beginning and an end. You can always take another route through the landscape, observing what it looks like at different times, from different angles:

> Granted we did not find the riches of which we had been told, we found a place in which to search for them ("Footprints 4").

How to Interpret Hypertext Novels?

Hypertext, as Ted Nelson defined it, means "non-sequential writing – text that branches and allows choices to the reader, best read at an interactive screen" (Nelson 1993: 0/2). Cybertextuality, in its turn, directs our attention to the ways texts function, to how they *do* things. What do we mean by "interpretation" when we are dealing with texts which are constantly in the middle of a process – either subject to readers' choices, or to programmed actions, or to both simultaneously? And is it possible at all to interpret something in which you have to be involved (if not immersed) as an active participant of the meaning production? Or is it the case that the distance necessary for interpretation kills the participatory process and thus, in a sense, denies the object of interpretation?

Tentatively we may assume that, taking into consideration the almost infinite variety in the field of hyper and cybertextuality, there is also variation in the interpretative activity. I will now compare *Califia* to the "classical" hypernovel (presented here in the form of Stuart Moulthrop's *Victory Garden* [1991]) from the viewpoint of interpretation.

Califia and *Victory Garden* exemplify two very different ways to use hypertextual structure in narrative fiction. *Califia* can be described, on a very basic level, as an archive. The archive is collected around one master story, the historical Califia saga. All the other narratives (including the real time narrative of Augusta) are just sub-stories in that saga. The archive is very open; it can be approached and used in many ways, and in many orders. However, the way one uses the archive does not alter the master story. The hypertextual structure allows, in the spirit of Nelson's definition, choices to the reader while it also serves as a platform for the multimedial contents of the archive. However, all this does not affect the interpretational activity in a radical way. The way the archive is structured and the devices for using it are a matter of usability rather than of interpretation. While reading, there is the movement from details to the big picture and back, but there is also the possibility to step back from the immersion and scrutinize the work in its entirety. As mentioned earlier, the exit point is to some degree only provisional, and the text encourages repeated readings (wanderings in the fictional landscape of *Califia*) – it is, however, clear that after some point only minor alterations are possible.

There is also the aspect of the fictional world's expansion or intrusion into the real world: the reader is asked to consult the documents in the Los Angeles Public Library, she is asked to contribute her own stories to the Califia crew etc. This way it completes the thematization of the hermeneutic interpretation at work throughout *Califia*. The reader enters the fictional world with knowledge of the real world – this knowledge then functions as the first framework through which the text is naturalized. When the reading proceeds, the autonomous laws of the fictional world presented are foregrounded, and the interpretative activity concerns mainly the relation of details and story fragments to the whole story. When the saturation point is reached and the reader exits the story world, it is once again compared to the real world. One more circle in the hermeneutic activity and the fictional world is integrated into the experiences of the reader, and it becomes a part of the reader's world. It always has the potential to affect the reader's worldview, and thus condition further experiences. In its extreme form, it could be argued that the hermeneutical interpretation is the effect the work has on the reader's understanding of the world.

With *Victory Garden* the situation is different. It cannot be satisfactorily seen as an archive. It is rather a machine or a system, which produces different stories. These different stories do not contribute to any master story. Furthermore, in many cases they are incompatible with each other. With a text machine like this the hermeneutic interpretation described above is not as easily employed. The details and story fragments cannot be integrated into a whole, or interpreted from the viewpoint of some big picture, because there is no big picture.[5] There are only alternative stories, and once you exit the story world, take the necessary distance to interpret the work, you can never know what the next event would have been, had you chosen to read just a little further. In this case there are two possibilities for interpretation. The first option is to treat that version of the work you have read as the sole subject of your interpretation. It may appear more or less fragmentary, but once you have decided this is all there is; it is always possible to construct interpretational frames which explain the fragmentary nature, and possible contradictions, of the narrative. However, there are some inherent problems with this kind of approach. The most important is the question of what we do with that kind of interpretation – after all, it is possible that no other reader ever reads the work the same way. There will be as many works as there are readers. Thus, the differences in interpretation are not primarily products of different interpretative conventions, but of a more fundamental order: they are interpretations of different works. This is not to deny the value or legitimacy of such an approach; we just have to make clear that in this case we are dealing

---

[5] With *Victory Garden*, there may be a possibility for a big picture (for a detailed analysis see Koskimaa 2001). I am exaggerating somewhat, for the sake of argument (but it is not hard to imagine a hypertext narrative larger and even more complex than *Victory Garden*).

with experiences that gain much of their aesthetic power through their (quasi) unique nature.[6]

The other possibility is to try and understand how the text machine works, what the rules and limits for the story production are. Once the mechanism is explained, it serves as a general model of which any single reading is just one possible actualization. This can be compared to the analysis of poetics, in which a set of common properties is "distilled" from a body of texts (the oeuvre of a certain author, genre, period etc.) Instead of "The Problems of Dostoevsky's Poetics," we could then scrutinize the problems of *Victory Garden*'s poetics. This means acknowledging the generative nature of hypertexts concerning the interpretational activity. By means of a meta-level interpretation, we can construct a common background to which any individual reading is compared. That way it helps us to overcome the solipsism described above. We can also give a meaning to the mechanism; part of the interpretation must be explaining why this particular mechanism is used and what is its statement and how it is functioning together with the materials subjected to it.

We now have two types of hypertexts: *Califia*, which is well suited to hermeneutic interpretation, and *Victory Garden* which is best suited for poetic analysis. These are both hypertexts which are clearly static in nature. With dynamic texts evolving in time, the situation is again different. They are best seen as historical events which must be more or less arbitrarily limited to comprehensible units, which are then interpreted in relation to all relevant circumstances, keeping in mind that they are only local interpretations of certain phases of ongoing processes.

Works cited

Aarseth, Espen (1997) *Cybertext. Perspectives on Ergodic Literature*. Baltimore & London: The Johns Hopkins University Press.
Bolter, Jay David (1996) "Ekhprasis, virtual reality, and the future of writing" in Nunberg, Geoffrey (ed.) *The Future of the Book*. Berkeley, CA: University of California Press, 253-272.
Coverley, M. D. (1997) "Elys, The Lacemaker", part of a collaborative Web work, Sanford, Christy Sheffield (ed.) *The Book of Hours of Madame de Lafayette*. <http://gnv.fdt.net/~christys/Coverley/elys_1.html>.
— (1999a) "Endless Suburbs", in *Iowa Review Web*. <http://califia.interspeed.net/EndSub/endless.htm>.

---

[6] Quasi-unique, since any particular reading of a hypertext can be repeated in exactly the same order. In this case, part of the work has gained an independent status; it has become a work of its own.

— (1999b) "Life in the Cohocolate Mountains", in *Salt Hill Magazine* #7. <http://www.hypertxt.com/sh/no7/choc/achoc.htm>.
— (2000a) "RainFrames: Poetry", in *Aileron* (Spring). <http://califia.interspeed.net/RainFrames/rainfr1.htm>.
— (2000b) "Fibonacci's Daughter", in *New River* #7. <http://www.cddc.vt.edu/journals/newriver/>.
— (2000c) *Califia*. Electronic text. Watertown, MA: Eastgate Systems.
Davis, Erik (1993) "Techgnosis, Magic, Memory, and the Angels of Information", *The South Atlantic Quarterly* 92:4, 585-616.
Eskelinen, Markku (1998) "Omission Impossible – The Ergodics of Time", <http://www.kolumbus.fi/mareske/>.
— (2001) "(Introduction to) Cybertext Narratology", in Eskelinen, Markku & Koskimaa, Raine (eds.) *The Cybertext Yearbook 2000*. The Research Center for Contemporary Culture Publications Series 68. Jyväskylä: University of Jyväskylä.
Foucault, Michel (1986) "Of Other Spaces", *Diacritics* 16:1, 22-27.
Harshaw, Benjamin (1984) "Fictionality and Fields of Reference. Remarks on a Theoretical Framework", *Poetics Today* 5:2, 227-251.
Jackson, Shelley (1995) *Patchwork Girl. By Mary/ Shelley & Herself*. Electronic text. Watertown, MA: Eastgate Systems.
Koskimaa, Raine (2001) "Reading *Victory Garden*" in Eskelinen, Markku & Koskimaa, Raine (eds.) *The Cybertext Yearbook 2000*. The Research Center for Contemporary Culture Publications Series 68. Jyväskylä: University of Jyväskylä.
Larsen, Deena (1996) *Samplers. Nine Vicious Little Hypertexts*. Electronic text. Watertown, MA: Eastgate Systems.
Luesebrink, Marjorie C. (1998) "The Moment in Hypertext: A Brief Lexicon of Time", in Grönbaek, Kaj & Mylonas, Elli & Shipman, III, Frank M. (eds.) *The Proceedings of the Ninth ACM Conference on Hypertext and Hypermedia*, 106-112. New York: ACM.
McClure, John A. (1995) "Postmodern / Post-secular: Contemporary Fiction and Spirituality", *Modern Fiction Studies* 41:1, 141-163.
Miller, Rand & Miller, Robyn (1993) *Myst*. Computer game. Broderbund.
Moulthrop, Stuart (1991) *Victory Garden*. Electronic text. Watertown, MA: Eastgate Systems.
Nelson, Theodore Holm (1993 [1981]) *Literary Machines*. Sausalito, CA: Mindful Press.
Pavel, Thomas G (1986) *Fictional Worlds*. Cambridge, MA: Harvard University Press.
Pold, Søren (1998) "Writing the Scripted Spaces", seminar paper in *Virtual Environments: Applied Aesthetics and the Information Society Summer School* (International Institute of Applied Aesthetics, Lahti, Finland 1998; forthcoming in the seminar proceedings).
Wortzel, Adrianne (1995) *The Electronic Chronicles*. Electronic text. <http://artnetweb.com/artnetweb/projects/ahneed/first.html>.

II
Internet Text

Underground Lies:
Revisiting Narrative in Hyperfiction

Richard Saint-Gelais & René Audet
(CRELIQ/Université Laval)

It has become something of a (postmodern) cliché to say that we live in an age of hybridization of genres and styles, of permeability of fields which the modernist tradition has liked to consider according to a logic of autonomy.[1] Given this context, it is hardly a surprise to note the attraction exercised by hyperfiction over researchers (but perhaps to a lesser extent over readers themselves, although it is still too early to say). Situated at the crossroads of computer science and literature, hyperfiction is often described as an exciting burgeoning artform which favors experimentation and innovation. Taking advantage of technical advances in programming and graphic design, it makes good use of the latest gadgets and the constantly renewed potential of computer systems. However, it is not certain that computer science and literature do equally well out of – and have an equal say in – this dual enterprise. If the computer characteristics of hypertext and hyperfiction have been widely studied by computer scientists and the authors themselves, their literary dimension remains a minor element in discussions and studies,[2] which usually seem to be based on the implicit postulate that "hypergenres" constitute the way forward for a literature which, in its written form, is a thing of the past having exhausted its possibilities. Hyperfiction, then, has not bridged the gap between the "two cultures" (many literary minds consider it to be a gadget possessing no literary value whatsoever), but has perhaps only updated the prejudices that persist on either side. We do not claim to be able to change this situation, but merely wish to propose a critical examination of one of the clichés, the one which consists of considering fiction from the privileged point of view of the narrative, as though the former could be reduced to the latter – and as

---

[1] Translated by Jean Valenti.
[2] See Ryan ed. (1999) for an example of such a perspective.

though hyperfiction's contribution could be reduced to simply multiplying possible narratives starting from a single work.

If we think about it, the term 'hyperfiction', born of the marriage between the qualifier "fiction" and the medium 'hypertext', reveals itself to be surprisingly apt at describing the works it designates. Indeed, it puts a greater emphasis on the elaboration of a fiction (rather than of a narration) in a context which breaks with the conventional linearity and uniqueness of literary works.[3] For the general conception of hyperfiction as a *narrative fiction* – which thus postulates an equation between fiction and narrative – appears to be, albeit hardly in a systematic way, an exaggeration. Of course, the prefix "hyper-" leads the reader to expect certain special characteristics, which may be modulations (or transformations) of the established conventions of literature. However, the fact that these (hyper)fictions obey the general laws of narrative seems to be taken for granted: the reader expects to find characters, actions, motivations and plots, the role of the "hyper-" limiting itself to complicating rather than questioning these facts. As for hyperfictional studies, they usually refer to those works in the literary field which multiply narratives or the possible readings of them,[4] and tend to neglect the attempts of writers, from Laurence Sterne to Harry Mathews, to consider fiction in a way that cannot be reduced to narrative in the strictest meaning of the word.

But hyperfictions, cannot always be reduced to hypernarratives, that is to texts offering diverse schemes of variation on a segmented narrative framework of events. This explains certain reading difficulties which are often referred to in empirical studies of hypertextual reading: these difficulties not only arise from the computer environment as such, but also from perplexity in the face of fictional discourses which wipe out plot or make it undergo transformations beyond mere fragmentation or the multiplication of possible narrative frameworks.

In order to put this hypothesis to the test, we will study two cases, each of which illustrates the way in which hyperfiction questions the idea of narrativity. The first case, *253*,[5] presents us with a stream of characters all of whom are aboard a London subway train at the same time, while the second case, *Lies*, leads us to constantly reinterpret the statements of a fiction built up from truths and lies. These texts – chosen for their heuristic quality rather than for their representative nature or esthetic value – will allow us

---

[3] It is true that "fiction," as an editorial category, essentially refers to novels. Nevertheless, common usage has preferred the term "hyperfiction" to other possibilities such as "hypernovel" or "hypernarrative," even if we do actually talk about interactive novels and narratives.
[4] Julio Cortázar's *Hopscotch*, for example.
[5] Available at <http://www.ryman-novel.com>; for screenshots of *253*, see contribution by Van Looy.

to better grasp the narrative expectations of the reader and their necessary reorientation in the face of certain hyperfictions. More precisely, they will enable us to show how fictional hypertexts influence the general conception of narrativity (and its reading parameters), since these texts cannot be reduced to textual jigsaw puzzles or narratives that the reader simply reconstructs in his own way.

253: *embryonic narrativity, or game of narrative hide-and-seek?*

From the start, Geoff Ryman's *253* orients its own reading. Possibly in the hope of remaining within the literary field (rather than a computer science or cybercultural domain), the author multiplies traditional generic indicators: *253* is subtitled: "a novel for the Internet about London Underground in seven cars and a crash" (home page); the hypertext's presentation states that: "This novel describes an epic journey from Embankment station, to the Elephant and Castle (...)" (why.htm). Suggesting the notion that this is a novel, a story recounting outstanding events, the paratext leads the reader to anticipate a plot, a conventional diegetic construction which takes place in the London Underground. However, Ryman's spirit of contradiction and ironic attitude, present throughout the work, are obvious as early as the presentation page, as he candidly admits: "Nothing much happens in this novel. It is ideal fare for invalids. Those seeking sensation are advised to select the End of the Line option." (why.htm) Overturning expectations, taking pleasure in deconstructing conventions (a novel recounts events spread out over time, linked by a chain of causality and centered upon one or several protagonists), the author lays claim to a documentary approach on the daily life of a big city, but only to immediately denounce it as an illusion and to mock the reader's voyeuristic tendencies: "Do you sometimes wonder who the strangers around you are? This novel will give you the illusion that you can know." (why.htm) A novel in which nothing much happens, or one which "describes an epic journey"... what tale, then, is being told?

The textual aspect of *253* makes it difficult to believe that an actual story is being told. This hyperfiction is principally made up of 253 texts corresponding to the 253 passengers (7 cars with 36 passengers each plus a driver) of a subway train in London. Multiplying the constraints, the author proposes texts of 253 words in which each character is in turn described in three ways: Outward appearance, Inside information, and What he/she is doing or thinking. Multiple hypertextual links are integrated into these texts, directing the reader towards other texts describing other characters.

These links leading from one character to another are like meeting places, crossing points which, of course, are akin to subway connections, which constitute not only the background of the fiction but also a metaphor for its very organization. The links serve mainly to teach us who is hiding behind the names mentioned in a text (by leading to the description of the character in question). Another effect is that they bring two or more characters together according to a looped or chain route. For example, the reader can discover which characters have links of one form or another to British Telecom. The meeting places vary enormously: they may be geographical markers, businesses or institutions, newspapers, etc. But we must note above all that these hypertextual links do not furnish the basis for generating plots and have more in common with intersections in set theory: we might learn, for example, that passengers x and y are, each in their own car, both reading *The Independent*, but this fact will not necessarily serve as the departure point for any new narrative development. The novelistic potential of these links (and the reader's expectations on this front) are thus constantly being nipped in the bud. *253*, then, takes the form of a descriptive file whose narrative component, if not absent, seems very slight: the fiction does not offer piecemeal stories, but rather countless pieces of story.

Considered from such a point of view, the descriptive aspect seems to be rather oppressive. Indeed, the compulsory three parts of each of the 253 texts list qualifying terms and offer minutely detailed descriptions of the actants. The first rubric generally proposes an external look at the character: supposed age, clothing, objects, probable employment, way of moving; the second, which adopts an omniscient perspective, reveals true age, employment, status and recent activities; the third grants access to the character's thoughts and relates his recent or present interactions. For we must not be allowed to forget that all these texts place their subjects in the same place at the same time: all these characters are described as they appear during their subway journey, on the line that goes from Embankment to Elephant and Castle, on the morning of January 11th 1995. This simultaneity, initially quite anti-narrative, surprisingly enough allows for certain interactions to be put into place. It is the third section of the character description, often longer than the two others, which allows for the plots to unfold. Offering a transcription of what he or she is doing or thinking, this part relates the situation in which the character finds himself; entering the subway car, choosing his seat, watching his neighbors, waiting for the station where he will get out, sometimes changing his mind about his destination... At times he will witness a theater play (88.htm), he will watch a pigeon which has inadvertently entered the car (133.htm), he will sing an accompaniment for an old woman who wants to dance (223.htm) or he will complain about another passenger's odor (72.htm). The action may become more complex: for example, the woman who meets a friend, both of whom are seen from afar by the first woman's husband (167.htm, 194.htm, 238.htm); two women who do not know one another meet and walk together towards the museum while talking of their passion for cats (80.htm, 95.htm)... Slight narrative developments can thus be observed by the reader who follows the links and reconstructs, piece by piece, the puzzle of a situation sliced up according to the different perspectives of the characters involved.[6] But this "puzzle" is deceptive: it never leads to more than a few reconstructions without much plot potential.

The epic journey announced in the presentation of *253* lies in a unique event, which involves all the characters described: the crash of the subway train at the end of the line. Never actually referred to in the character descriptions, it is retold seven times in the texts called "End of the Line" which close the list of characters in each car and which refer to the disastrous fates of certain characters.[7] An event which is both dramatic and spectacular, the crash itself does not figure in the story: the reader is presented with a *fait accompli*. On seven occasions the crash is reported as an isolated incident, subsequent to the story fragments but with no explicit causal link to them. Only a few ironic comments appear here and there: one of the victims is a man contemplating suicide who wonders how his loved ones will still be able to claim under his insurance policy (101.htm); another has been robbed earlier in the day and does not believe that two serious incidents can take place in the same day (48.htm); still others have changed their minds about their destination and have remained on the train. But are these episodes, when taken together with the final crash, enough to allow us to speak of a narrative?

This question can be asked in a general manner of all *253*: does a combination of different points of view of the same fact produce a story? Do various narrative segments (the telling of past events, of funny occurrences, meaningless coincidences, etc.), once they have been brought together, create a narrative text in the same way as a novel does? The answer is linked to how the reader navigates his way through a hypertext, how he reads it. The manner in which this work is to be consulted is broadly

---

[6] To this form of narrativity is also added the descriptions of characters where their recent experiences are related, thus providing a second-degree narrative: the character thinks about what happened to him that morning or the day before, telling, via the omniscient narrator, the story of what occurred. For example, a love story between a woman and her half-brother (224.htm) or the difficult relationship between a son and his father (103.htm). These texts thus appear as autonomous short stories.

[7] Hence the fact that those readers seeking sensation are advised, in the presentation, to go directly to texts.

framed while remaining fairly unrestricted: advice on how to read abounds, as do the many possibilities for exploration. A Journey Planner, a stylized image offering indications and several links to the more or less important episodes of the hyperfiction, opens the whole. Passenger lists for each car are available, indicating name, position in the car and a brief résumé (2 or 3 words) of their thoughts or actions.[8] Each character description (duly numbered) offers, at the bottom of the page, links to preceding and following passengers, as well as others to the car map or the Journey Planner. Faced with this freedom and the multitude of possible readings, the reader can also follow the links at random, clicking on to the character whose name or two-word description intrigues him. Or, in a compulsively systematic way, he can read each notice in turn, in numerical order (and therefore one car after another according to the position of each character).[9] Surprisingly, this is probably the reading which enables the greatest understanding of the various events, in spite of (or perhaps thanks to?) a high incidence of redundant information.[10] An event linked to a few neighboring passengers is thus understood thanks to the different perspectives on offer, each of which is often incomplete; so, the reading of the "End of the Line" is made easier by knowing the preceding actions of the passengers involved. A linearity of the whole is created. The descriptions appear to be more systematic and less troubled by secondary facts in the first cars, as though in an attempt to make it easier to manage the text's structure. The middle car texts include events which divert the attention previously targeted on each character. See, for example, the subway theater group (96.htm). The disorder reaches its peak in the seventh and final car, where a party is taking place involving a series of eccentric characters. This could be read as the apotheosis of a long adventure, but if, and only if, the hyperfiction has been explored in a linear way. In this perspective, we can note that certain ways of exploring hyperfiction (albeit not all) favor reconstructing narrativity through the meanders of the text.

But the story remains, on the whole, hard to read: a bunch of episodes graft one onto another to form a coherent universe which is more simply grasped in a continuous reading but still does not constitute a complete and

---

[8] Note that, in some cases, the characters' positions allow the reader to understand certain situations.
[9] There is no opening text, if not for the Journey Planner which does not favor the choice of any particular segment, apart from those of the first car if the numerical order is to be respected.
[10] And we might suppose that this is, grosso modo, the order of writing. Certain signs would seem to indicate as much. For example, a woman (40.htm) insults a man who smells (39.htm); her words are initially reported in the text of the man's other neighbor (38.htm), they are completed in the text of the insulted man (39.htm) but are not in the woman's text (40.htm), since it is assumed that the reader is aware of them, having been reported twice...

global narrative.[11] Furthermore, an important paratextual framework brings to mind the fictional dimension of the text due to the series of footnotes which render the boundary between the fiction and the referent more problematic. These notes show how the fiction is anchored in reality (giving the meaning of the name of a certain building which really exists, pointing out that a particular commercial space is now abandoned or that a certain person has now entered politics), but at the same time, they remind us of the imaginative element introduced by the author who invents a stream of characters placed in equally fictive contexts.[12] On the one hand, contemporary London is constantly represented, as are the customs and specificity of its inhabitants (habits, typical attitudes, ethnic mix); on the other, the author explicitly notes the fictive nature of such a place or such an institution, sometimes in order to deplore the fact that it does not exist in reality. The fiction is constantly being constructed and deconstructed, numerous imaginary characters rub shoulders with others called John Kennedy, Margaret Thatcher (who worries she will be mistaken for the real one) and Anne Frank.[13] A second level is added to the fiction, that of the "Mind the Gap" theater group, performing sketches in the subway cars without most of the passengers knowing, a group which is trying out an amateur named Geoff Ryman...

This play dimension of the fiction confirms the author's strong position as he completely masters the universe he animates – hence the game of fictionalizing reality (places, buildings, people) and the multiplication of the traces of this fiction-under-construction. "Godlike" (why.htm), Ryman proposes a certain representation of reality as he perceives it but, more than this, as he can (re-)produce it. This is done by mixing elements from reality with characters who are either partly or wholly invented – just as the director of the "Mind the Gap" theater group is inspired by a "real" subway passenger to create his own character (87.htm, 124.htm). A composite entity, this represented reality, rather than taking the form of a continuous story, presents the necessary fragmentation of events involving a large group of individuals. The only way, therefore, to represent this *mise*

---

[11] Contrary to many hyperfictions (including *Lies*, which will be examined later), *253* does not in fact possess alternative diegetic frameworks: all the events take place in the same possible world.

[12] We must note Ryman's admitted intention to mislead his reader: "I promise that some of the information in these footnotes will be deliberately, willfully WRONG." (ftnt46.htm)

[13] The text even goes so far as to confirm that it is the real Anne Frank, who is unaware that she is the young Jewish girl made famous by her diary. Note the replacement of the trains leading to the concentration camps by the subway train, as well as an implicit play on words: everything occurs as though the text were trying (successfully!) to derail the reader off the tracks.

en discours of a fairly complex network which profits from hypertext's characteristics while favoring ellipsis and fragments, is through description. A look at contemporary society, *253* integrates – to its advantage – the widespread discourse on the spatiality of the electronic medium: its slogan, "In cyberspace, people become places" (home page), justifies the use of the subway train and its seats, of the spatial inscription of the subway which crisscrosses the city. And the spatial and visual dimension, so self-evident, is translated not by the interaction between characters but by their representation, as obvious as possible, each text thus proposing a hypotypose where language, almost collapsing under the evocative effects of the figure, is constantly brought to the fore by Ryman's metafictional devices. Fiction as representation must necessarily annex anecdotes and coincidences[14] which furnish the image of the world being constructed; however, these narrative fragments never succeed in coming together in order to form even the most tenuously continuous narrative. This interactive novel thus asks the reader to rebuild, piece by piece, a universe: perhaps a reader may question himself at the end of his exploration as to the actual links between these numerous employees of British Telecom who are unaware of one another's existence. Perhaps he will try to imagine Tom McHugh's fate, dead drunk but who escapes unscathed from the collapsed subway train... From this perspective, this hyperfiction's interactivity may lie in the call to the reader's imagination faced with all these narrative beginnings, this incomplete information, these slices of life of characters to whom we are repeatedly introduced. Obliged to fill the multitude of narrative gaps, which are constantly remarked upon by the author, the reader seems to succeed in at least letting him be carried away by the representation of a certain fictive universe, even if he cannot produce hypothetical scenarios. The term "novel" which Ryman proposes is perhaps not meant ironically, but is rather an invitation to consider the novelistic potentialities in a perspective which is not limited to narrativity in the strictest sense of the word.

Lies: *as I lay lying*

Considered on the strict basis of its hypertextual structure, Rick Pryll's *Lies*[15] appears more conventional than *253*. This hyperfiction is made up of forty-one segments (each one numbered), most of which are attributed to the same narrator, a young man who relates diverse micro-episodes of his love life. The journey through *Lies* begins with segment 1 to which the

---

[14] "The world is as full of coincidences as *253*." (ftnt186.htm)
[15] Available at <http://www.users.rcn.com/rick.interport/lies/lies.html>.

home page gives access; then, a series of binary choices are offered to the reader who can thus progress towards one of three endings (segments 32, 41 or 42).[16] *Lies* does not include an overall plan, nor one obvious path. However, it is possible to gain entry to any segment by opening the corresponding address.[17] By having recourse to this stratagem (and by arming himself with patience), the reader will manage to reconstruct a global map of the choices offered to him; it is at this point that he may notice that certain segments are missing and, above all, that the hypertext contains the equivalent of a secret chamber: no key grants access to segment 11, which can be read either as an alternative beginning or as a stage in the already started narrative,[18] and which opens onto two segments (6 and 13) which can also be reached by using the keys (respectively: 1—> 5—> 6 and 1—> 12—> 13). We must note that segment 11 does not contain any particularly meaningful revelation (compared to what can be learned from other segments); the discovery of this secret segment, if ever it occurs, does not affect the global understanding of the "story" but draws the reader's attention to the formal architecture of this hypertext.[19]

The fictional frameworks produced by the different readings of the hypertext remind the reader of the rather twisted love relationship between the narrator and his mistress, both of whom are anonymous and not exactly faithful to one another. Speaking strictly of its content, *Lies* puts us in mind of a soap opera, with the dramatic reversals (of the x deceives y/y deceives x variety) experienced by its idle protagonists who spend their time traveling, dancing and drinking wine or rum and coke. But things are in fact a lot less simple, for *Lies* contains many a trick whose combined effect is to completely destabilize the reconstruction of the fictional universe. The reader often sets out from the premise that the hypertextual structure will offer him the possibility to explore the virtualities of a fictional universe

---

[16] This number is explained by the fact that the numbering of the segments includes a certain amount of deliberate errors: there are no segments numbered 2, 3 or 4; on the other hand, there is a segment 99.

[17] For example, to access segment 33: <http://www.users.interport.net/~rick/lies/lies33.html>. However, the fact that certain numbers do not correspond to any segment transforms this system into one where the reader must grope along the best he can.

[18] Its text reads: "I used to go dancing just about every Thursday. The truth is, that is how I met the woman I live with now. Aside from all our other problems, we really love to dance. Dance and drink rum and coke."

[19] Contrary to the numbering of the segments, it is not certain that this curiosity is intended. Nevertheless, it constitutes an interesting concretization of the idea of hidden recesses which is undoubtedly an obsession for many a hypertext reader (see, for example, Douglas, 1994: 172). In this respect, *Lies* is like *253* which also contains some surprising discoveries, such as the notes to the notes (see in particular 134.htm, ftnt134.htm and ftntb134.htm). It is interesting to remark that the reader of the book version of *253* (Ryman 1998) cannot but see the footnotes which the electronic version permits to maintain out of sight until the reader follows the link.

(defined by a certain number of starting points: characters, situations, places) by creating diverse narrative destinies. But there is no such premise in *Lies*, whose fiction possesses the particularity of constantly unmaking itself as the reader reconstructs it, not only from one narrative framework to another, but even within the same framework.

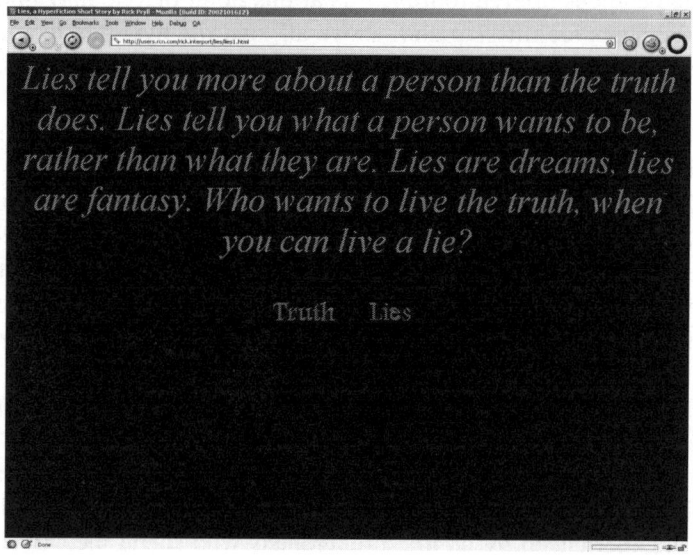

The first (and most immediately perceived) trick in *Lies* is that the keys are named "TRUTH" and "LIES." It is not uncommon for hypertext keys to be semantically oriented (the most banal strategy being to present an utterance or a key-word which indicates in advance the direction the plot will take). But *Lies* differs by making its keys into metafictional operators which assign a truth value to the narrative segments they open: a segment reached by clicking on TRUTH will be held as true (in the fictive universe of course), while a segment reached via the key LIES will be considered as false. We can see that *Lies* exploits what Lubomir Dolezel (1998: 145-168) calls the authentication function, thus creating a perverse effect. In a "standard" hyperfiction, each narrative framework is considered, for as long as it is being read, as authentic, and mutually contradictory events are separated into different frameworks. In *Lies*, the reader (unless he keeps to the option TRUTH, in which case he will create a trivial and disappointing story) is constantly called upon to coordinate pieces of stories which are not necessarily contradictory as far as their content is concerned, but which are brought into question each time they are indexed under LIES.

The hypertext's organization complicates matters even more. The succession of keys produces a rather disturbing recursive effect: should the indexes TRUTH and LIES be interpreted absolutely or in relation to the preceding segment? Is a segment marked TRUTH which follows a segment marked LIES true, or true in relation to the preceding segment (thus false, unless the latter were itself followed by another segment marked LIES)? From here on, the treelike structure of the network leads to extremely complex ontological constructions: there is not a true narrative framework and a false framework, neither a true framework and several false frameworks, but rather an interlacing of versions of fluctuating authenticity which correspond to more than doubtful "stories."[20] How is one to keep the thread of indexes in a (typical) sequence like 1—> TRUTH—> 12—> LIES—> 13—> TRUTH—> 16—> LIES—> 17—> LIES—> 19—> LIES—> 18? This embarrassing situation may be perceived as a fault in Pryll's hypertext, which introduces an interesting variation but does not allow the reader to take into account all its consequences and ramifications, unless he transforms himself into a logician.[21] *Lies* thus reveals itself to be quite frustrating, since it prevents its readers from keeping in mind all the components, both narrative and metanarrative, of a single framework. The perplexity induced actually blocks the "free" exploration of possibilities which are simply too complex for the reader to effectively follow them.

Without necessarily defending Pryll's hyperfiction, we must however note that the reader is not obliged to devote himself to various calculations of logic which would fast become fastidious: he can follow the narration, while constantly being forced to remind himself that the unfolding plot is ontologically unstable. Just as he cannot take into account *all* the values of truth, neither can the reader disregard the fact that the hypertext constantly denounces its own articulations as false or at the very least dubious.

These considerations of *Lies'* structure should not, however, prevent us from examining the segments themselves (and their linking), which are remarkable in that they contribute to the metafictional dimension of this

---

[20] We must add that the architecture of these links can sometimes produce nonsensical effects: both options leading out of segment 14 direct the reader to the same segment, number 15; this segment's status therefore becomes absolutely undecidable. The respective tenor of segments 14 and 15 does not allow the reader to determine whether the second one confirms or invalidates the first one.

[21] To complicate matters even more, it is (theoretically) possible to read the TRUTH and LIES buttons as a choice of labels for what one has just read: thus interpreted, the buttons become a game of "if you think you've been told a truth (or a lie), see what unfolds from this premise".

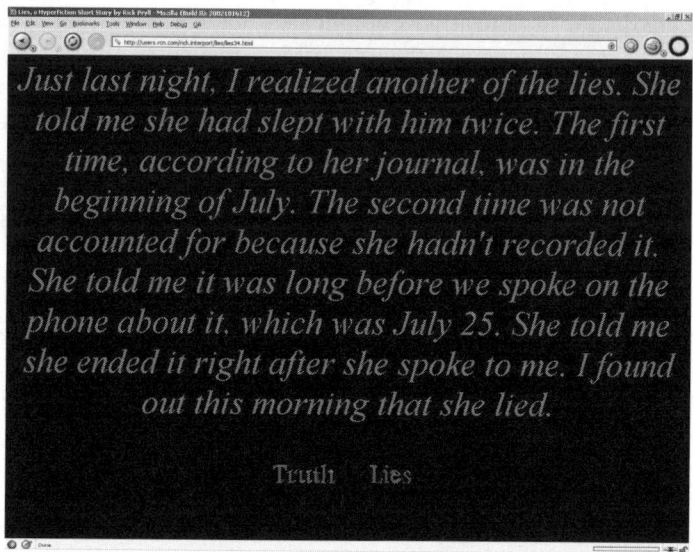

hyperfiction. Certain segments are purely narrative and present slices of story. These, for example, (respectively 5 and 27):[22]

> We have been seeing each other for one year as of last night. One year ago, we met in a dance club. She had invited me secretly, as a secret admirer. I had no idea who she was, but I went anyway. She came up to me and asked if I wanted to dance. I told her that I don't dance I drink. She bought me a rum and coke.
>
> Last summer we were apart. I worked in Germany, and she didn't work, here. We wrote lots of letters, we proclaimed our love for each other, and we both had summer lovers.

Nothing, if not of course the index keys, allows us to doubt the veracity of these episodes, which are inserted into certain readings giving them a definite narrative consistency.[23] But if the reader reaches segment 13 (accessible with equal ease from segment 5 or 27), the narrative suddenly rocks on its foundations:

> Oh, I should explain. We have code words for lying. We call it "dancing." And "to enjoy rum and coke" is to enjoy telling the other about your lies and crying over it. These codes help us to be more open with each other. It's hard to tell someone that they're lying, but it's easy to say "you're dancing."

---

[22] The readings allow the reader to access either of these segments without going through the other; certain readings lead from 27 to 5 (via intermediary stages) but not the opposite.

[23] For example, 27—> LIES—> 28—> TRUTH—> 29—> LIES—> 30 or 5—> LIES—> 8—> LIES—> 9—> LIES—> 7.

Equally, segment 14 (which can be reached from segment 13) reveals that the summer lovers are actually diary entries about sexual fantasies. We can thus imagine a reader following this tale of infidelity quite trustingly, and another (or the same reader, in a subsequent reading) who discovers that the story is not what he thought it was... We must underline that these plays on truth and lies are tightly linked to the mechanism of the TRUTH and LIES keys: on the one hand, they put a metafictional emphasis on the story itself; on the other, they are subject to and may be affected by it. As he accesses segments 13 and 14 by the LIES key, the reader may ask himself whether the revelations about the lovers' code is not itself a lie on behalf of the narrator...

Other segments mix up matters even more, particularly number 41, which seems to tower over all the others and to offer the real truth:

> You want the truth? The narrator is me. The other main character is my girlfriend, with whom I now live. Our summer lovers were real, but they had different names. The journal stuff was true, too. Those books are forbidden reading now, since we talked the whole thing to death.

But how can we trust this if we reach this segment after segment 39[24] ("This card is a little hint. The author reaches down into his diorama and changes the course of everything"), whereby segment 41's revelation becomes the explicit extension of a mere writing decision?

Lies is then, in the end, a "maddening hypertext," which is less interested in elaborating a narrative (or range of narratives) than it is in constantly destabilizing this narrative. Many hyperfictions are content to explode a narrative into several divergent versions, protected from one another and each one dominating the path in which they are developed. *Lies* does not even give access to alternative versions, but shatters each one, retracing its steps in order to exacerbate the fiction's uncertainties. Fictive situations, keys, metafictional indications: everything converges so that the reader is left asking where is the truth and where is the lie. Everything also converges to leave him asking which element has a hold over the others (must he interpret the fictive situations in the light of the metafictional indications, and the latter in the light of the keys, etc.?). What is at stake in *Lies* is not, therefore, the reconstitution of a narrative puzzle, but rather an interrogation of the respective powers of the text and the hypertextual mechanism.

---

[24] By following the reading 39—> LIES—> 18—> LIES—> 41.

Conclusion

When faced with hyperfictions, two temptations seem to lie in wait for readers and critics, and so much so that they alone monopolize the terms of the theoretical debate underway for several years now. The first is the optimistic (if not indeed euphoric) conception of the hypertext: for those who hold this notion, hyperfiction offers a potential multitude of narratives, among which the reader can (and must) choose the one which his interests, or the whims of his explorations, end up creating. Hyperfiction will therefore succeed in liberating the reader from the tyranny of linearity (and of the single narrative, imposed once and for all by the writer). Promoted to equal status with the author, the reader can exercise his freedom by crisscrossing the network as he wishes and by elaborating his own narratives starting from the possibilities offered by hyperfictions, which can henceforth be seen as the materialization of Eco's open work or Barthes' writerly text.

The second temptation is that of pessimism. It underlies an important number of empirical studies based on the reactions of readers whom researchers subject to hyperfictions. These readers are frequently disappointed not to find narratives in due form, or otherwise experience great difficulty in reconstituting them; they judge that the suspense is often wiped out by the hypertextual structure which causes them to bounce from fragment to fragment and quickly dilutes the interest which, in their eyes, the plot is supposed to arouse.

It is clear that while the optimistic theories often proceed by theoretical a prioris and that the pessimistic studies confront this optimism with the harsh realities of reading, both types of approach are united in that they suppose an equivalence between fiction and narrative. The promoters of liberty imagine readers who construct their own narratives out of the fictional patchwork; the skeptical researchers observe readers who are in despair for not being able to do so. The notion that (hyper)fiction can escape narrative's grasp simply does not seem to have been considered, unless in terms of fragmentation (hyperfiction as puzzle) and of multiple reconstructions. With the idea of parallel narrative frameworks, this notion ends up by making hyperfiction an unexpected application of the semantics of possible worlds as imagined by Leibniz and theorized by contemporary logicians. The variety of adventures can thus be understood according to a certain number of stable elements (characters, starting points, etc.) opening up into a layering of developments which are each supposed to obey the logic of the plot. However, the frustration of some readers shows that this is not always the case: hyperfiction may belong to the realm of fiction but not of narrative thus understood. The complication it entails does not consist of multiplying narratives, but of putting fiction together according to different principles of organization, for example the saturation and reticulation in *253*, or the incessant self-questioning of the fictive facts in *Lies*.

In this context, the readers' frustration appears very much to be a sign of resistance, but we may wonder whether this is a result of the hypertextual structure as such or a type of fiction which escapes from the categories usually associated with the narrative. It would be vain to underestimate this reticence and to imagine that hyperfictions on their own can unleash a revolution in the way in which readers conceive of narrative and fiction. Yet we would not conclude that the narrative is the natural way of fiction (and, even more, that it is the only way), and that any deviation from this constitutes at best a curiosity for specialists. Without wiping away traditional expectations altogether, hyperfiction proposes a reading environment different enough from that of the book so that readers may immediately envisage a renegotiation of the relationship between the support, the discursive organization and the fictional framework – a renegotiation where the computer environment is not reduced to the puzzle-maker's saw but where it contributes on an equal footing, using its own means, to the renewal of both fiction and reading.

Works cited

Dolezel, Lubomir (1998). *Heterocosmica. Fiction and Possible Worlds*. Baltimore: Johns Hopkins University Press (coll. "Parallax").
Douglas, J. Yellowlees (1994). " 'How do I Stop this Thing?': Closure and Indeterminacy in Interactive Narratives", in George P. Landow ed. *Hyper/Text/ Theory*. Baltimore: Johns Hopkins University Press, 159-188.
Ryan, Marie-Laure ed. (1999). *Cyberspace Textuality: Computer Technology and Literary Theory*. Bloomington and Indianapolis: Indiana University Press.
Ryman, Geoff (1996). *253 or Tube Theatre, a novel for the Internet about London Underground in seven cars and a crash*. <http://www.ryman-novel.com>
— (1998). *253, the journey of 253 lifetimes: the print remix*. London: Flamingo.

Stealing or Giving? On Raymond Federman's & Anne Burdick's *Eating Books*

Jan Baetens
(K.U.Leuven)

Do not read this text?

In this article, I would like to tackle an idea which has become one of the cornerstones of contemporary academic doxa on electronic literature: the idea that the digital version of a traditional text cannot be (and can never become) a good, i.e. a challenging or simply an interesting piece. Indeed, many authors stress the gap between, on the one hand, an electronic text which is nothing more than the electronic translation of an already existing printed version,[1] and, on the other hand, a digital text properly conceived and elaborated from the very beginning as an original work taking into account the distinctive characteristics of the new medium such as non-sequentiality, interactivity or the blurred frontier between the verbal and the visual (for a survey of this discussion, see Vos 1996).

Although I share a preoccupation with specificity and medium-related writing and thinking,[2] a purist interpretation of this principle would entail that a number of very appealing digital texts are discarded due to their being insufficiently distant from a previous, traditional version. The example I would like to comment on in these pages will suggest that the claim of 'digitextual' specificity is not as simple as one might think. Hence, any serious scholarship on hypertextuality ought to include a reflection on the way classical, i.e. textual features are reworked in a hypertext regime. Furthermore, one should not forget that the specific features of a new

---

[1] Available at <http://www.altx.com/ebr/ebr7/ebr7.htm>
[2] Nothing more, and often even less, since it has been observed that the electronic version of traditional literature systematically erases the material features (e.g. typeface and layout) and the peritextual surroundings (e.g. the illustrations and the jacket blurb) which have always played a paramount role in the individualization of texts.

medium are never fully known in advance: media are no universals, no essentialized and dehistoricized structures existing independently from their concrete realizations (Cavell 1979). Media historians have demonstrated that each new medium is in fact born twice: a first time when its technological infrastructure is discovered, a second time when its emerging uses are being – always temporarily – institutionalized (Gaudreault & Marion 2000).

An anti-hypertext?

"Eating Books" tells a simple anecdote.[3] The story goes that when Voltaire met Newton in London, he noticed the presence of a book in the pocket of the latter. Observing that the book seemed to be half-hidden, Voltaire is supposed to have said: "to steal a book is not a crime as long as the book is read." Raymond Federman's text itself is a very short extract from *Loose Shoes*, a 'novel' recently published in print form (Federman 2001) and released earlier as an e-book on the site of The Buffalo Center for Electronic Poetry (Federman 2000a). However, the version I will discuss here is not a fragment of the complete book (whatever its publication form may be), but the independent short story issued by *Electronic Book Review* in 1996 (Federman 1996), more particularly the short story as it was graphically designed by Anne Burdick (whom I consider a co-author of the work).[4]

"Eating Books" is a work that, at first sight, does not correspond to the basic standards of what one expects from a digital text (even apart from its very theme, which deals with, as I will analyze in more detail later, with the stealing, eating, and reading of books).

First, the work is deeply rooted in textual culture: it is a linear piece of writing, which avoids any experiment with the search for spatiality, simultaneity and most of all de-linearization in the electronic writing space: since "Eating Books" unfolds itself in a teasingly (or aggressively) linear way, one could even argue that it actively resists the tendency to the spatial inscription of texts in hyperspace.

Second, the textual features of the work are designed in such a way that (typo)graphically speaking the link with older forms of writing is clearly

---

[3] It cannot be repeated often enough that thinking, no less than writing, is an activity with a material foundation, making it, whether the agent likes this or not, a materialist activity. The following quotation by Mallarmé: "Ton acte, toujours, s'applique à du papier..." (your act [of writing, JB] always applies to paper), ought to be kept in mind by those who think that the electronic environment is bodiless and dematerialized.

[4] Anne Burdick is the graphic designer of the electronic book review <http://www.electronicbookreview.com>, in both its former and its present form.

marked: the letters of "Eating Books" are not exclusively set in modern typefaces; when the narrator includes supposedly 18th century quotations the letters resemble very ancient forms of calligraphy and handwriting.

Third, there are not only references to traditional print culture and traditional writing, but also to what our phonocentric tradition considers the very basis of every writing: orality, speech, physically uttered words. Not in the sense that "Eating books" is both a reading piece and an audio-book, a multimedia performance one can read as well as listen to, but in the even more classical sense that the structure of the text radicalizes the most profound feature of oral speech: its passing-by, its temporality, its ephemerity. The words and sentences that build up "Eating Books" literally adopt the form of a string, of a line which one has to read from left to right in a narrow horizontal window (a 'window in the window' pops up when the text is opened and the reader has to use the scroll bar to make the text creep from right to left on that strip), and once the text has disappeared on the left hand side of the screen, there is no way to reread the vanished fragment.[5] Just like the product of the human voice, unless registered and archived by a machine, can never be heard again, the portion of the text that has been read also disappears after its utterance, i.e. after its reading by the clicking reader. From the viewpoint of iterativity, the electronic version of "Eating Books" seems

---

[5] If the reader wants to reread what he has erased, he is obliged to launch the whole text from the beginning. For a more radical example of a text whose rereading is made impossible by its very program, see John Cayley's *Book Unbound* (Cayley 2001)

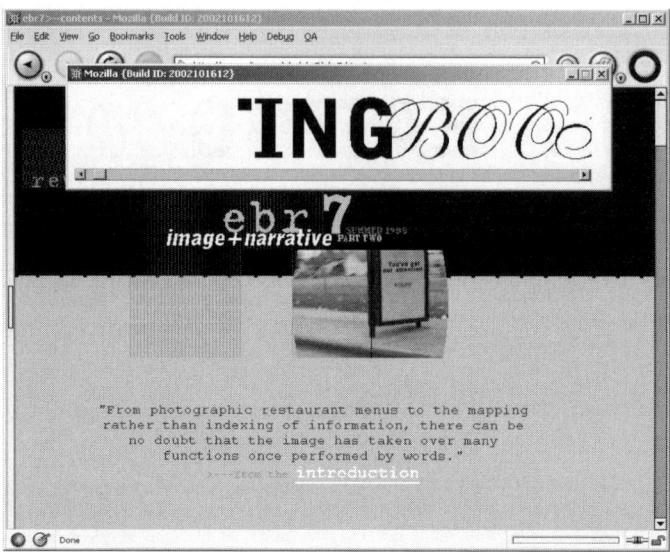

to be regressive in comparison with traditionally written language: its words cannot be retrieved ad libitum and they seem to be as ephemeral as the spoken word which writing – traditional or electronic – purports to fix eternally. Fourth, the work does not allow its reader much freedom or initiative, and even the interactivity allowed, given the fact that the reader has to scroll the text from right to left, seems a crude parody of the reader's manipulation of the electronic word in hypertext. In "Eating Books," navigation (let alone surfing…) does not seem to be a major priority.

In short, even though there are other examples of heterodox use of digital text, most readers will agree that "Eating Books" features most of the characteristics which our current doxa confidently considers alien to 'true' hypertextuality. Moreover, the very 'simplicity' of the work can be read as a sardonic critique of one of the least contested key aspects of contemporary hypertext, which is generally considered fascinating to the extent that its technical structure is 'difficult' (or 'new'). Minimalism has a bright future in digital text, where generally speaking one can observe, both in popular knowledge and in academic writing, a systematic overvaluation and overappreciation of technology and technological complexity, at the expense of content and technological/structural simplicity.[6] The curious thing with Federman, then, is that his enthusiastic leap into the digital text in the second half of the nineties, does nothing to include the physical

---

[6] See for instance Gaggi (1997: 126) for a comment on the gap between the technical complexity of Michael Joyce's *Afternoon*, and the great simplicity of the message its electronic links and hyperstructures want to make clear: the fact that the reader makes the story…

elements of staging that the electronic medium makes available today: Federman does not play with images, nor does he add an audio-level to his creation. The digital text he produces is a simple, plain, linear text (its linearity is a symptom of the fact that the text 'regresses' to an earlier, oral phase, rather than 'progressing' towards the newer forms of writing), and the more 'technological' it gets, the more the resulting text seems to be just a word-chain, a piece of linear writing. This choice of absolute simplicity is all the more astonishing since other works of Federman in print form have often followed different directions. His second novel, for instance, *Take It Or Leave It* (Federman 1976), opens with a metafictional[7] comment upon the double reading, linear and syntactic on the one hand, visual and non-syntactic, on the other, that one can make of this book in which all pages tend to have a different and specific lay-out. And the 'recyclopedic'[8] project carried out by a trio of Federman scholars, *Federman From A to XXXX* (McCaffery 1997) is a printed one-volume encyclopedia in hypertext form, where the reader cannot 'properly' read (sometimes not even one entry after the other), but where he has to surf and cross-over from one section to another in a way which is as perturbing to the linear logic of writing as any multi-story and open-ended hypertext fiction.

The strategic importance of a work such as "Eating Books" is to make a plea for an equilibrium between form and content, between medium and message, i.e. for a type of reading where one tries to interpret the merits of a hypertext in function of the way it realizes – successfully or not – its global, all-embracing project. It is to this project that I will now turn again, before continuing the interpretation of "Eating Books."

A dialogical return of the linear

As I have argued before, "Eating Books" alludes, in an apparently paradoxical way, to two different, but in fact not antagonistic modes or models of narration: the written, which belongs to typographical culture and high-art tradition, and the oral, which belongs to the world of performance and whose register is considered more colloquial. This ambivalence is a major feature of Raymond Federman's work, since the publication of

---

[7] Metafiction: on Federman's use of this term, see "Surfiction: A Postmodern Position" (Federman 1993: 35-47).
[8] By this – evidently autoreflexive – 'porte-manteau' word, the authors mean the combination of encyclopedia and recycling, two major features of the author's work. Just as Federman's writing, this survey of his work does not avoid any sensitive subject, nor does it refuse any type of reuse (a ludic form of quotation and rewriting, which Federman himself likes to call 'playgiarism').

his first novel, *Double Or Nothing* (Federman, 1971) until his most recent experiments with electronic writing (Federman 2000b). Indeed, although Federman mainly writes novels and short stories, the almost direct communication with the reader (or with the narratee, more precisely)[9] which is pursued (and often obtained) in almost every page of these books, is not a clean, bodiless, typographical one, but a physical communication, without distance, hands-on if one might say, with a voice, a face, a body, a presence. Verbal and narrative communication do not only obey the ideal 'typographical' model (McLuhan 1967, Postman 1985), but also follow the logic of the oral and visual interaction between a person on stage and his audience. Although typographically mediated, Federman's texts are not 'typographical' products, but staged experiences; they are events or performances in their own right rather than their transcription, and they ask not so much to be read as to be performed by a physically present author and a willingly or unwillingly cooperating, equally physically present reader.

Of course, this tradition of mimed oral storytelling and communication is very old (it is, in contemporary literature, the tradition of the 'skaz' as studied by Russian Formalism (Titunik 1974)), and of the dialogical imagination in literature (Bakhtin 1981): the implied presence of a reader prevents the narrator's discourse from remaining monological, and the fact that this reader is also imagined as a listener tightens, reinforces the dialogical perspective of a text. The fundamental commitment of Federman's work to the notion of dialogue (both literally, as a fictive discussion with an audience, and metaphorically, as a plea for heterogeneity) explains why "Eating Books" makes such a curious choice in favour of linearity, i.e. against everything which should make digital text a seductive solution for modernist writers. By stressing the intense and inexorable linearity and sequentiality of his hypertext, Federman does not 'refuse' the hypertextual nirvana of unlimited textual possibilities, but reaffirms the global coherence of his writing project. It is the craving for a mixed, i.e. explicitly written as well as implicitly oral mode of writing, which helps him to keep the text as linear as possible even in a hypertextual environment. Indeed, by creating a digital text which is just one running string of letters, words and sentences, Federman manages to preserve even in digital text the continual influence of the oral on the written mode (and by stressing the spatial direction of

---

[9] As theorized by Gerard Prince (1973) and other narratologists, the difference between author, implied author and narrator is reflected by a similar distinction between reader, implied reader and narratee. In the case of Federman, the very distinction of these agents and levels is intensely and dramatically thematized and problematized in the work. For lack of space, I will not explicitly discuss this issue which is crucial in the work of Federman (for more details see "Federman on Federman: Lie or Die" (Federman 1993: 85-104).

the reading – we have to scroll from left to right – Federman makes a similar point). In other words, the electronic medium is not only used but also and most importantly modified (the disappointing 'under-use' of the medium is the modifying element here) in such a way that the basic oralization of the written word remains intact even in the hypertextual mode of writing.

That the story not only deals with the 'stealing' of books, but also with their 'eating' (following a move to which I will return), can only increase the orality of the story. And once again, it is the typography which underlines this dimension. When one starts moving the text from right to left on the screen, the very form of the sentences and the letters of the words produce the visual equivalent of a text that is gradually swallowed: the text is literally eaten, both because the string of letters enters the mouth as a spaghetti-like worm and because the typographical font used for some words is so baroquely curled that its letters make us think of the pasta one turns around on a fork before consuming it. All this may seem strange to the reader unfamiliar with Raymond Federman's work, but it suffices to have one single glance at *Double or Nothing*, Federman's "noodles book" (the narrator pretends having locked himself up with enough noodles to write the book without ever having to leave his room) to know that the physical equivalence between the text and the theme is not just the result of the heated imagination of the reader: In *Double or Nothing*, Federman's typographically most innovative work, the position of the words on the page has the ambition to make the reader see a dish of noodles on every page.

Moreover, the link between 'stealing' books and their 'being eaten' makes the concrete starting point of the story ("If it ever becomes necessary for you to eat a book, out of despair or out of some primal need, then eat the telephone book, for it is the only book in your library which came free. Except, of course, the books you stole"), and this linking does not only affirm the global correspondence between 'stealing' books (in the case of Federman, this means: quoting from books without providing any sources) and 'eating' them (absorbing their knowledge, their power, their fun, their laughter). It also brings to the fore that the eating of the text essentially has to do with the activation of its oral dimension: indeed, the first book which comes to mind when one is thinking of 'eating books' is the telephone book, i.e. the book whose function is to facilitate an oral communication with a physically absent and generally invisible addressee, just like what the narrator of Federman's books always tries to obtain through the typographical manipulation of the text (one could add that the telephone book is also the book where one looks for a restaurant phone number...). And of course, it stresses the almost synonymous relationship of reading and eating, and announces what will be at the heart of this text: the identity of writing and surviving. But before one can get to this point, one has to further analyze the importance of the line and, more generally speaking, of linearity in "Eating Books."

The strategy of digression

One has to ask what the profound meaning of Federman's linearity is, beside the function it plays in the 'skaz'-like intertwining of oral and written language, and in the blocking of some hypertextual 'seductions'. The particular type of linearity displayed by Federman's text has nothing to do with the simple, linear succession of the verbal elements, but obeys a specific literary strategy of teasing and withdrawing: Federman does not so much tell a story than he tries to defer it. His main scope is that of the eternal digression, a mechanism hardly studied in classical rhetoric, since it exceeds the microscopic level of the word and the sentence so much, but well-known by narratologists. As far as Federman is concerned, digression is used so systematically, in his whole oeuvre as well as in "Eating Books," that one ought to consider it a real constraint,[10] i.e. not a local figure but an over-all structure whose application both hinders and blocks the author (a constraint preventing him or her from writing 'naturally') and enables him or her to invent and write what could not have been written otherwise (a constraint is, as Raymond Roussel and the Oulipo-authors after him recognized [see for instance Bens 1981], an inspiration-machine, aimed to help writers to overcome their writer's block).

The global digressive structure of "Eating Books" is easy to sketch: the basic anecdote is told in three small segments, which appear more or less in the beginning ("to steal a book"), in the middle ("is not a crime") and at the end ("as long as one reads the book"). But by virtue of the digressive movement of the whole of the text these three segments are separated by a large number of what structuralism called "catalyzers" (Barthes 1977), that is, elements with are inserted in the text around its 'kernels'. Indeed, the reader of "Eating Books" is told, after an introduction which seems to go in several directions, that:

---

[10] See Schiavetta (1999 and 2000) and, more generally, the works collected in the journal FORMULES (1997-) (see www.formules.net).

(a) the sentence in question was in fact pronounced in another language (in French: "voler un livre"),
(b) it was said by Voltaire (and this apparently innocent detail introduces a new shift in the reading process, since one can notice, as long one has a minimal knowledge of French, Federman's mother tongue[11], that 'voler' and 'Voltaire' have their first syllable in common, 'vol', the noun-form derived from the verb 'voler', which means both 'to steal' and 'to fly', while the second half of Voltaire's name, '-taire', which means 'to keep silence (on something)' also suggests a direct relationship with the theme of stealing and concealing),
(c) it was said by somebody who was a notorious 'anti-Semite' (which makes him virtually an... unreliable narrator),
(d) it was told to someone, Newton, whom Voltaire seems to suspect of having stolen the book (while the reader of course starts to suspect Voltaire of having done the same with the books he must have in his pockets too),
(e) it is also said here and now to an anonymous addressee, a 'you', which in the light of the phonic and linguistic shifts throughout the whole story, can also be read as a paronymic form of 'Jew' (and this relative equivalence of 'you' and 'Jew' reinforces of course the game the narrator is playing with the narratee: if the reader is addressed as 'you', and is thus close to the 'Jews' Voltaire hated so much, then this reader can only become suspicious of what the French philosopher is supposed to have said, and sympathetic towards the narrator who is... stealing a sentence from Voltaire!).

The unraveling of the word-strip's digressive structure brings out a first thematic and formal network which gradually focuses the text on the relationship between the two actors or agents at first unequally represented: I and you (I say 'unequally' because of the limited material interactivity of the work, which the reader – 'you' – can only unfold without any further opportunity of manipulation or retroaction). That the construction of such a network is the very purpose of a digressive reading, which does not leave the digressive parts of a work aside but, on the contrary, let them play a central role in the reading process, has been usefully studied by recent scholarship on the mechanism of digression, most notably in the book by Pierre Bayard on the famous digressions in Proust's *Remembrance of Things Past* (Bayard 1996). As Bayard argues, digressive and non-digressive parts

---

[11] I will not discuss this in full detail, see "A voice within a Voice" (Federman 1993: 76-84). and the interview published in Baetens (2001). *Loose Shoes*, the book of which "Eating Books" is just a fragment, goes very far in this bilingualism, and this is of course what enables me to pick up at least some small aspects of it.

of a work can display a vast array of common features, and if this is not the case, the need of coherence is so strong that this set of shared properties will inevitably be constructed by the reader. In some cases, the relationship between 'core text' (kernel) and 'digression' (catalyzer) can even be inverted, that is when the reader starts discovering that by establishing the secret links between the digressive and non-digressive parts, the first happen to contain the essential elements of the text.

Eating or Being Eaten in Cyberspace

As far as "Eating Books" is concerned, such a reorientation of the reading is not hard to motivate. Indeed, thanks to the fact that Federman's digressive strategy is not just a figure, but a constraint, it is perfectly justified to single out some 'details' hidden in the digressive meanders of the texts as imperative elements. One has to go back to the text in order to unearth some of these topics, but not without forgetting that they will also have to be interpreted in the light of the electronic form in which we read the work.

One does not need to have a profound knowledge of Federman's work to know that, just like most of his other writings, "Eating Books" is inextricably linked to his War experience. Repeatedly, he has recounted what he has gone through when the Nazis came to arrest his father, mother and two sisters, and how he escaped deportation to Auschwitz where his entire family died. Being one of the most eminent (but also one of the most eminently courageous and comic) representatives of so-called Holocaust fiction, Federman's work presents the very act of writing as a survival technique: the survivor's tale is not only a testimony of things gone and lives destroyed, but also the very proof of an inextinguishable lust for life.

In our western tradition, the book is considered the very basis of our civilisation; it therefore constitutes a survival kit on its own. Yet Federman, with his typical sardonic humor, reinterprets the cliché of the book as spiritual nourishment in a very down-to-earth and bodily way: books become food, and help avoid starvation (what counts in that respect is their weight, and maybe the taste of their pulp, their ink, their glue, certainly not the sublime meaning of their words). Simultaneously, 'to eat' is a word itself, that is, an object which can enter a network of relationships with other words. We already saw that the name of Voltaire, via a bilingual pun, is not unrelated to the theme of theft. We can now add to this type of reading some new couples such as 'to eat' and 'to hate' (in the text Voltaire is called several times 'Jew-hater', and one should notice, in this short text full of phonic and graphic shifts and correspondences, the movement between 'eating' and 'hating'). Such a link is not a play with words. On the contrary, it indicates to what extent the meaning of a word or a theme can be modified by very small transformations: if the verb 'to eat' is close to the verb 'to hate' one possible conclusion could be that this relationship does not work one way and that, conversely, 'to hate' can also be read as 'to eat', an interpretation which throws a new light on what happened before and during the camps: first it was books that were burned, eaten by fire, then it was the people who read them... Hating turns into an act of physical disintegration and annihilation of the other (which can of course also take the form of 'vomiting', but this issue is not explicit in "Eating books").

Yet "Eating Books" is not just yet another – in this case rather indirect or metaphorical – survivor's tale. It is a survivor's tale in digital text, and any consistent interpretation of this story should try to catch why digital textuality matters, and how it does so. I believe that what is at stake in the 'digitextual' turn of "Eating Books," and which Burdick's graphic design admirably brings to the fore, represents its major characteristic: the stylistic mechanism of digression. By making a systematic use of digression, Federman turns his narrator into a kind of male Sheherazde. He writes and tells in such a way that he can make things last, the most essential thing being of course double: his own voice on the one hand, and his audience on the other. "Eating Books" shows the degree to which it is important and difficult to communicate with an audience, with a 'you' that must be convinced again and again, and that can virtually mutate into an enemy of the 'I' (there is in this text a sinister labyrinthine knot of 'I', 'you', 'Jew', and of 'hating', 'stealing' and 'eating' suggesting that the narrator's voice is safe nowhere, unless it can go on telling and writing).[12]

The disappearance of his text once it has been read is the most secret fear of the narrator, which constitutes the unstable ground on which "Eating Books," and probably all of Federman's work, is built. And this fear is exactly what is materialized by the graphic design chosen by Anne Burdick, who manages to present the act of reading as an act of cannibalism, and to show that reading a text is not only a way of communicating with the author but, at least virtually, a way of destroying him.

---

[12] A slightly different reading of "Eating books" could emphasize the analogies between Federman's text and the 'joke', more specifically the 'shaggy dog story'. In his reading of *Tristram Shandy*, Samuel Weber writes that: "(f)or Freud, the shaggy dog story was one of the borderline cases of the joke, in which the narrator tells the joke directly at the expense of the listener – who can only "revenge" himself by in turn becoming a first person, a re-teller of tales" (Weber 1987: 69). It is very clear that the reading of "Eating books" as a 'shaggy dog story' would reinforce not only the irony of the Federman's text, but also its dialogical dimension.

At the same time, however, the digital form of "Eating Books" also suggests that this killing of author and text is a form of suicide, and thus of the danger of listening to a stranger's voice. In the same way, 'to eat' and 'to hate' are mutually interchangeable, while 'to eat' has almost contradictory meanings (to destroy something or somebody else, but also to sustain oneself), the sense of 'hate' loses its simple meaning, the one the reader can find in a dictionary, in order to become a word in which the demand for love is obliquely inscribed.

Works cited

Baetens, Jan (2001). "La visualité d'un roman parlé: *Take It Or Leave It*", followed by "Raymond Federman à la question", in *Rivista di Lettere Moderne et Comparate* 2001-2, 211-230.
Bakhtin, Mikhail (1981). *The Dialogical Imagination*. Austin: University of Texas Press.
Barthes, Roland (1977). "Introduction to the Structural Analysis of Narratives", in *Image-Music-Text: Essays Selected and Translated by Stephen Heath*. Glagow: Fontana/Collins.
Bayard, Pierre (1996). *Le Hors-sujet. Proust et la digression*. Paris: Minuit.
Bens, Jacques (1981). "Queneau oulipien", in Oulipo. Atlas de littérature potentielle. Paris: UGE (10/18), 22-33.
Cayley, John (2001). "Book Unbound", in *Indra's Net*. <http://www.shadoof.net/in/>.
Cavell, Stanley (1979). *The World Viewed*. Enlarged edition. Cambridge, Mass.: Harvard University Press.
Federman, Raymond (1971). *Double Or Nothing*. Chicago: Swallow Press.
— (1976). *Take It Or Leave It*. New York: Fiction Collective.
— (1993). *Critifiction. Postmodern Essays*. Albany: State University of New York Press.
— (1996). "Eating Books", in *electronic book review* 7 (special issue on 'Image + Narrative', guest-editors Steva Tomasula and Anne Burdick). <http://www.altx.com/ebr/ebr7/ebr7.htm>
— (2000a). *Loose Shoes*. Buffalo, NY: Electronic Poetry Center. Available at: <http://epc.buffalo.edu/authors/federman/shoes/>
— (2000b). <http://wings.buffalo.edu/epc/authors/federman/>
— (2001) *Loose Shoes*. Berlin: Weidler.
Gaggi, Silvio (1997). *From Text to Hypertext. Decentering the Subject in Fiction, film, the Visual Arts, and Electronic Media*. Philadelphia: University of Pennsylvania Press.
Gaudréault, André & Philippe Marion (2000). "Un média naît toujours deux fois", in *Sociétés et Représentations* 9 (special issue on "La Croisée des médias"), 21-36.
McCaffery, Larry, Thomas Hartl & Doug Rice (eds) (1997). *Federman From A to XXXX. A Recyclopedic Narrative*. San Diego State University Press.
McLuhan, Marshall & Quentin Fiore (1967). *The Medium Is the Massage*. Harmondsworth: Penguin.

Postman, Neil (1986). *Amusing Ourselves To Death. Public Discourse in the Age of Show Business*. New York: Viking.
Prince, Gerald (1973). "Introduction à l'étude du narrataire", in *Poétique* 14, 178-196.
Schiavetta, Bernardo (1999-2000). "Toward a General Theory of the Constraint", in *electronic book review* 10 (special issue on Constrained writing, guest-editor Jan Baetens) Available at: <http://www.altx.com/ebr/ebr10/10sch.htm>
— (2000). "Définir la contrainte?", in *Formules* 4, 20-55.
Titunik, Irwin Robert (1974). *The Problem of skaz in Russian Literature*. Ann Arbor: University Microfilms (PhD dissertation Berkeley, 1963).
Vos, Eric (1996). "New Media Poetry. Theory and Strategies", in *Visible language* 30-2 (special issue on "New Media Poetry"), 214-233.
Weber, Samuel (1987). *Institution and Interpretation*. Minneapolis: University of Minnesota Press.

One Must Be Calm and Laugh:
Geoff Ryman's Web Novel *253* as a
Hypertextual Contemplation on Modernity

Jan van Looy
(University of Leuven)

In this paper we will investigate how *253*[1] uses hypertext to reflect upon modernity through the thoughts and concerns of two hundred and fifty three people in the London Subway. First, we will try to situate *253* as an Internet Novel. We will investigate generic claims and tackle the question if the Web should be considered a medium or a deliverer. Second, we will describe the hypertext framework and we will attempt to find out how this structure bears on the manner in which the narrative is experienced and organized. Third, we will differentiate between a number of narratological devices and try to see if and how the way in which the story is laid out results in a new type of narrative. Finally, we will see how the thematic construction of the novel is grafted upon both hypertext and narrative structuring and how it is therefore excellently placed to question its own modernity and that of the narrative world it creates.

253 as an Internet novel

If we start from the full title, i.e. *253 or Tube Theatre, a novel for the Internet about London Underground in seven cars and a crash*, there are already three important clues about the generic claims of Ryman's work. Very prominent, and even more prominent in the alt-text[2] of the logo, is the

---

[1] Available at <http://www.ryman-novel.com>
[2] In hypertext markup language (html) you can add an 'alt' attribute to the image tag. This is the text that appears when the user has disabled images in the browser or (in Internet Explorer) hovers the image with his mouse. For people who use text-only or speech browsers (e.g. disabled people), it is the only indication of what the image contains. The alt-text for the logo on the first page (index.htm) reads "253 or Tube Theatre, a novel by Geoff Ryman."

term 'novel'. *253* is no ordinary novel however, it is a novel for the Internet. Finally, in the first clause of the title, *253* is designated as being Tube Theatre. In the next paragraphs, we will investigate these three claims.

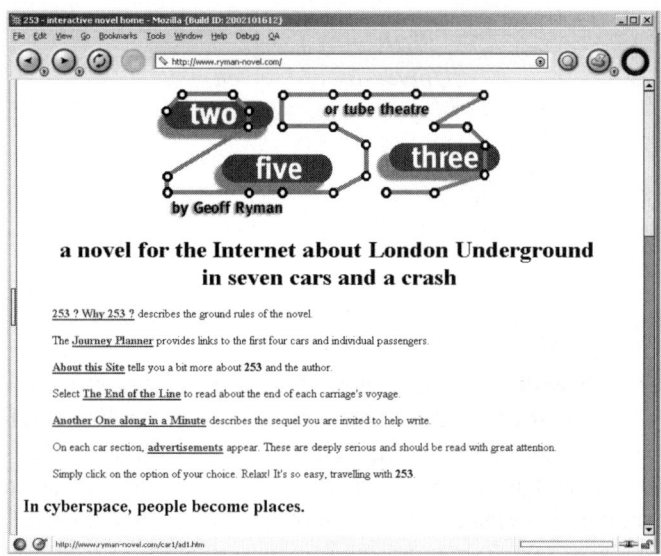

253 relates to the term 'novel' both in its adjectival and its nominal meaning. Ryman's work is meant to be something innovative, a new type of fiction written for the Internet. Containing approximately 350 pages (files), it is one of the longest multi-linear fictions online. It deals with the life and sometimes the death of 253 people on a Bakerloo line train in London. *253* is "[a]n extended fictional work in prose (…) in the form of a story" (Lewis 2001). In February 1998, Flamingo (London) published an adapted book version of the Internet novel. In this paper, we will be dealing with the online version only.

As Wilf Voss noted in his 1998 interview with Geoff Ryman, *253* "was consciously written to exploit the new possibilities for writing which the Internet [the World Wide Web, jvl] offered" (Voss 1998). When we look at Ryman's novel today (2002 vs. 1997) from a designer's point of view, we do not just see the Web, but we see the Web as it used to be in the mid-nineties. Very little graphical design features have been used in order to allow people with a slow dial-in connection to load the pages at a pleasant speed. The tables used to present the car maps in a more or less iconic fashion, all have a text only alternative available. Ryman emphasizes the fact that *253* is a novel for the Internet. The term mostly used to designate "non-sequential writing" (Nelson 1993) in the nineties, i.e. hypertext, is strangely absent. Nevertheless, *253* very much conforms to what Nelson had in mind when he coined the term and described it as "text that branches and allows choices to the reader, best read at an interactive screen." *253* is not called an Internet novel because Ryman is unfamiliar with hypertext or its aesthetics. In an interview with Leonie Winson, he describes how he experimented with HyperCard. "[I]t never really clicked (...) the story lines were too ambitious... everything happening in Manhattan Kansas in a day in 1844, and again in 1877 and again in 1903" (Winson 2000). One possible solution as to why *253* is not described as hypertext is that Ryman, being a Web designer, is very much aware of the fact that HTML[3] is only a derivative of the hypertext idea. Although it does allow for non-sequential text by means of hyperlinking, it is very much restricted to unidirectional one-to-one linking. The term 'Internet novel' may have seemed more appropriate than 'hypertext novel'.

Linked to the first page, there are a number of announcements or advertisements, i.e. meta-texts stylized like the cheap ads one finds in the London subway. They allow the author to comment on his work. The first announcement promises to deliver the user from literary embarrassment. "How often have you been embarrassed when serious fiction is discussed at the office?" (ad1.htm). An embarrassing situation is sketched: "You're at a dinner party. Your partner for the evening says, 'Forrest Gump is a Christ symbol'. You realize that you have missed the point again." Then the new miraculous technique is introduced: "*253* uses the miracle of information technology to ensure that you can follow the main themes and relationships that link the text. Without even having to remember who the characters are!" By displacing the literary discussion to a cheap ad, Ryman is able to give his opinion from behind a veil of irony. "*253* – a world of success and romance could be yours for the price of [a] phone call."

The second announcement is titled "Become a writer in your spare time" (ad2.htm). It describes a word game in which the user should take one word from each passenger page, e.g. the ninth, and build a new one. This may be a sneer at post-structural literary theory, where it is sometimes claimed that authors only rewrite. "[Treat] words as things, [move] them into place and [count] them. That is all that writers do!" The style and setting of the announcements contribute to the tongue-in-cheek undertone. "You'll have a fun hobby and will impress

---

[3] HyperText Markup Language, markup computer language devised by Tim Berners-Lee around 1989. Together with the HyperText Transfer Protocol (http), it formed the basis for the success of the WorldWide Web (www). *253* is entirely written in html.

your friends." On the other hand, if all an author does is counting and moving words, then perhaps one day she will be replaced by a computer. This is yet another claim often made by all too optimistic theorists and mockingly addressed by the ad.

The fourth announcement is even more explicit in its attack on literature and jargon alike. It advertises a guide to homely English. "Ashamed by your English? You're chatting up a bird at the bar. You say, 'The beauty of the Web is that you can utilise ftp, pdf or even Telnet through one interface'" (ad4.htm). Then, the ad proposes a calculation determining the complexity of the language used. Some examples like Proust, Terry Pratchett and the Sun Newspaper have been added. By juxtaposing Proust and the Sun, Ryman is ridiculing his own proposal, but he also points out one important characteristic of *253*, i.e. its use of plain speech and its ironic references to high literature. Again, this may bear on the fact that Ryman is trying to keep aloof from the hypertext theoretical approach.

The seventh announcement pretends to be an oracular device: "[t]he 253 Way to Knowledge" (ad7.htm). It describes a game in which the player should think of a problem, flip a coin eight times and check the passenger corresponding to the binary number thus obtained. This may be a reference to the (post-structural) theoretical concept of 'play' (Fr. 'jeu': movement, fluctuation of meaning) sometimes applied to hypertext as 'playfulness' (see e.g. Landow 1997). *253* is not a prototypical game however. The user is not the main protagonist and her actions do not constitute the novel's course or storyline. In other words, the interaction within *253* is limited to the reading process itself and the choice of a reading path. "About the only reader motivation that *253* shares with a good game is curiosity: where do we go next?" (Ryman in Winson 2000).

Beside the alliteration in the phrase 'tube theatre', there are also thematic echoes of drama in *253*. In car number three there is a performance of "Mind the Gap" taking place. Paying customers follow a number of actors performing routines on different trains in the London Underground. Being probably one of the most amusing and most sophisticated scenes of the entire novel it will be dealt with more closely when discussing hypertext syntax. Another example is Ms Susan Wheen, a drama student pretending to read *Clean and Jerk*, a best seller about female weight lifters. She is actually part of an advertising campaign paying actors to visibly read magazines or books in the underground.

Conceptually, the manner in which *253* approaches the act of storytelling bears similarities to the way in which theater translates narrative to performance. The fact that so much emphasis is placed upon characterization and interaction, rather than development of personas gives the novel a theatrical atmosphere. There is a continual sense of spatial proximity. There is no fourth wall. The user can choose which character to look at by clicking a hyperlink, just like she can choose an actor to focus on in a theatrical play. Furthermore, the laws of simultaneity apply. Several things are happening at the same time, some actions being experienced by only one person, others by an entire wagon. Although the different pages can only be read sequentially, the experience for the user is one of simultaneity. The lack of linearity produces a sense of looking around and experiencing simultaneous events.

Dramatic irony is facilitated by the hypertextual format of the novel. One event can be described by different passengers and in some cases these perspectives clash. Amanda Stinton and Gary Collier, a married man, are having an affair. Gary has told his wife he is leaving her while the reader may already know Amanda has decided to end the relationship. This results in a very theatrical scene.

> Gary gets off at Lambeth North. Two cars ahead, out comes Amanda. He saunters up behind her. "Boo," he says smiling.
> "Oh. You, is it?"
> "Sorry about Sunday. I got something to tell you," he says.
> "So have I," she says.
> They both speak at once. He says, "I told Toni. I'm leaving her." She says. "It's over Gary."
> Both of them stop, and stare. They don't move as everyone else walks by. (44.htm)

Of course, this effect could also be produced without the hyperlink, but the interaction provides an extra dimension, a sense of involvement unequaled by a linear description. "The links make irony very, very easy. It's almost too powerful a tool" (Ryman in Grossman 1997). It should be noted, however, that although *253* bears resemblance to drama, it also makes extended use of narratological devices like omniscience and focalization (cf. infra).

253 as an idea space

Ever since the early days of the Internet, geography and motion have been a source of inspiration for coining new terminology. People do not speak of 'contacting servers' or 'loading, processing and displaying HTML files'; they rather say they 'are on the information highway', 'go to Amazon' and 'spend some time in the CD-section'. The hypertext structure of *253* is equally based on the principles of geography and motion. While entering the novel, the user is steeped into the atmosphere of a London subway station. There are advertisements, which you can either walk past or glance at absent-mindedly. A journey planner and car maps cry for attention and strangely familiar voices sound from the loudspeaker. Although immersion (Murray 1997) is no primary goal in *253*, it is used to clarify the spatial metaphor used for structuring the fiction. "Usually the primary metaphor for fiction is temporal, the flow of time, although there is a spatial element. Here you're exploring the simultaneity of something, mainly spatial" (Grossman 1997).

Space is used both as a structuring device and as the running metaphor for the novel. On the first page there is a brief reference to the notion of cyberspace. "In cyberspace, people become places" (index.htm). This may be a reference to William Gibson's *Neuromancer* (Gibson 1984) in which the term 'cyberspace' was coined as a virtual space in which the mind is freed from the body. Similarly, *253* attempts to create a textual space in which the illusion of transparency is held up. The user is invited to travel through the minds and ideas of two hundred and fifty three people sitting in a train that is about to crash. Wathagundarl is a beautiful black woman who possesses supernatural powers.

> Watha is increasingly aware that she is a character in a work of fiction. She knows that no train actually crashed on 11 January 1995. Everything around her keeps breaking up into letters and code.
>
> The code breaks into numbers, which decay further into a blizzard of zeros and ones. They slip down wires like a dose of Novocain through nerves, to be reassembled (251.htm).

Like Case in Gibson's *Neuromancer*, Watha senses the virtual space around her, the blizzard of zeros and ones. In *253* many scenes give the user a sense of looking at a scene from the past, frozen and open to be explored and interpreted.

To prevent *253*'s three-dimensional text from becoming a labyrinth, it is structured by numbering in an almost obsessive fashion. "Numbers (...) are reliable. So that the illusion of an orderly universe can be maintained, all text in this novel, less headings, will number 253 words" (why.htm). Hence the title of the novel. As explained earlier, the number 253 refers to the number of people a Bakerloo line train can transport. All 252 passengers plus the driver have one page containing 253 words. "It's difficult to be tragic (...) in a universe where you only have 253 words to describe everybody" (Ryman in Grossman 1997). First, we will deal with the organizing principles of *253*'s hypertext framework itself. Then, before we move to narrative syntax, we will go deeper into the role links play in both the navigation and the generation of meaning within the novel.

253 contains a number of unique pages, e.g. the title page (index.htm), one where the structure is explained (why.htm) and one about the design team and the author himself. "All material on this site is copyright. I love you, God loves you, but you have no right to re-use or redistribute any of this material" (about.htm). One peculiar entry to the novel is the journey planner (home.htm). It consists of a visual map inspired by London underground maps containing links to the different cars and to some key-nodes linked to themes developed in the novel. There are seven car maps, each linking to 36 passengers, seven announcements and seven pages describing the crash for each car independently, they are titled "End of the line."

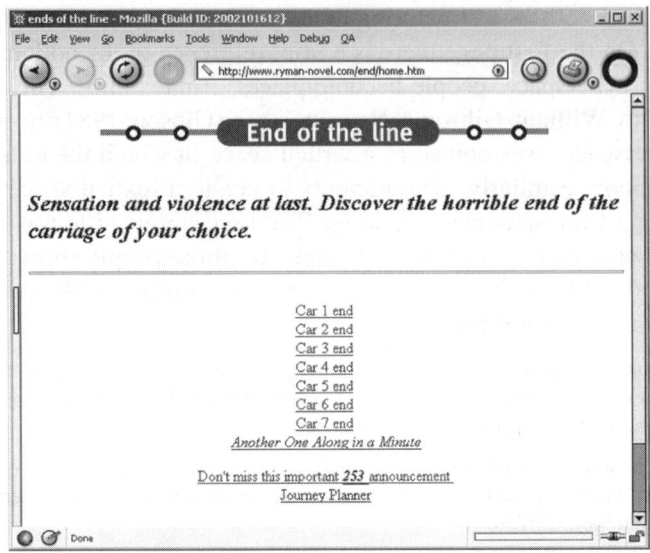

In the past, hypertext has been described as the equivalent of a book containing footnotes, whereby the latter were supposed to become superfluous in electronic media (see e.g. Landow 1997). Although *253* is a hypertext, it contains no less than 115 references to footnotes. One reason is probably that Ryman had difficulties keeping to his own rigid structure for the novel, and wanted to dwell on certain subjects. Another reason could be that he keeps to book terminology for convenience sake, to facilitate the adaptation of book readers to the new format. However, this does not alter the fact that the term 'footnote' is meaningless in an electronic environment like *253*. First of all, *253*'s footnotes are not found at the foot of a page. Second, they are not just notes, but full pages juxtaposed to their parent, making them simply another page in the Web. Ryman knows this and plays with his format. He debunks his own terminology by placing footnotes within footnotes (ftnt186b.htm, ftnt36.htm) and by linking pages through footnotes (ftnt94.htm).

The number of entries to the novel is vast. Depending on which link the user follows, she is taken to a different passenger page. Within the series of announcements (cf. supra) there are two thematic links leading into the body of the novel. Below links to car maps and the journey planner there is a table of contents at the bottom of the introductory page (index.htm). Even the interview by Grossman (Grossman 1997), which is situated within a separate domain, provides links to the passengers being discussed. Moreover, there is no overall climax in the novel. The fact that the train is about to crash is announced in the subtitle. Consequently, the work's decenteredness allows the user to commence reading at any point in the novel, and leave without the feeling of having missed something. Statistics seem to confirm this. There have been "a good number of accesses, which show most people are reading a substantial number of characters, say about [ten]" (Ryman in Winson 2000).

Why force such a rigid structural framework onto such a flexible medium? Why limit each passenger page to the meaningless number of 253 words if you then need footnotes to get the message across? This fact alone undermines the possibility that theoretical conviction is the reason. Ryman is not simply setting constraints due to artistic considerations like e.g. the Oulipo poets (Matthews & Brotchie 1998). Reducing a page to a certain number of words does not pose a constant constraint upon the author. Rather than steering the process of writing, it kills each story just when it is beginning to develop. This turns Ryman's restrictions into a handicap, rather than a constraint.

It seems that the structural and the narrative framework has been chosen for purely practical reasons. First, one of the major objectives of the novel is to provide the reader with a constant sense of space, of location, of orientation. Both the maps and the numbering allow the user to virtually visit a train in the last few moments of its existence. Very closely related to the orientation argument is the fact that a clear-cut structure makes it easier for the book-reader to adapt to multi-linear storytelling. It reduces cognitive overhead and removes the lost in hyperspace trap (Keep 1995). Moreover, it gives the user a sense of equal treatment of the characters. The illusion of an orderly universe is maintained. Furthermore, the dilemma of whether to follow an inline link (cf. infra) or not would be more prominent and disturbing on longer pages. With the current structure, a user can read the page to the bottom and then pick one of the inline links, which are one screen above at the most. Finally, text is inherently linear. To allow a hypertext to truly give a sense of multi-linearity, breaking up into fragments is the only option.

Passenger pages in *253* contain both inline links, i.e. linked words or phrases in the text, and navigational links at the bottom, i.e. links to the previous and the next passenger, to the car map and to the journey planner. In most cases this distinction corresponds to that between words that yield (Joyce, 1990) and pragmatic commands (Tolva, 1995). Inline links can also contain geographical references to other passengers, e.g. "the woman next to him..." The latter do not allow for much semantic play. Knowing the structure of the novel, the user will expect to arrive on a page dealing with the woman sitting next to the passenger about whom she is reading presently and she will probably be right. As for words that yield, there are sometimes interesting shifts of meaning contained by the link. The anchor on the word "terror" in the following sentence leads to a specialist in video surveillance systems. "May lives in terror" (13.htm). Semantic shifts in *253* are almost always metonymical. This contributes to the down-to-earth storytelling and unpoetic feel of Ryman's novel and again cognitive overhead is reduced.

253 is self-contained as far as linking is concerned. On the first page (index.htm), there are some four links to Web awards *253* has gained in the past and two links to reviews of the work (of which one seems to have disappeared in the meantime). In a footnote to the explanation of the novel, there is one more external link advising the reader to leave if he wants to "go somewhere sensible" (ftntwhy.htm). In HTML, every link is unidirectional. This means that if you make a link to a page somewhere on the Web, there is no other way of integrating a way for the user to return than to kindly ask to push the back-button at the end. Moreover, many pages on the Web constantly change addresses and content, making it impossible to include them into a coherent web. All this brings about that online fictions have not yet had the possibility to make use of the primary reason Tim Berners-Lee invented the World Wide Web in the first place (Berners-Lee, 2000), i.e. linking of different texts.

Finally, there are two special types of links that deserve our attention. First, in *Hypertext 2.0: The convergence of Contemporary Critical Theory and Technology* Landow claims that full hypertextuality depends on the presence of the possibility of one to many linking (Landow 1997). One source anchor, e.g. a word or a graphic, should be able to point to several target pages. This would allow the author to translate more complex semantic shifts to links. Indeed, such linking would improve the navigation of *253*. For example, the semantic link "neighbours" could very well be translated into one-to-many linking. Ryman has solved this problem by inserting an intermediary page showing a car map. The consecutive clicking of "car map" and then one of the neighboring passengers could therefore be seen as a surrogate for a single one-to-many selection.

String-to-string linking, i.e. linking a source phrase to a target phrase instead of a target page, seems to be a failure from the point of view of the user. She is literally thrown into a body of text without a starting point or a direction other than the source anchor. Moreover, most browsers have a very ugly way of jumping to an inline anchor. They simply scroll down until the line containing the target anchor is at the top of the window. This implementation seems to be the result of a very naïve conception of textuality. In particular, it is presumed that a textual entity has no context. The sentences coming before the target anchor are simply cut off by the top of the window. This results in confusion or even misinterpretation of situations in the novel. One possible solution for the user is to scroll back to the top of the page each time the target anchor is inline, which of course neutralizes the difference between ordinary and string-to-string links. Moreover, when there is not enough text beneath the target anchor, the browser is unable to scroll down. Instead, it stops somewhere in the middle of a page without giving a clue as to where the target is situated. An arrow pointing at the target anchor would probably be a more elegant solution for the browser, because it would allow displaying the phrase in its context and it would dispose of the need to scroll down to it.

In most traditional hyperfictions the principal motivation for using links is loose associative thought (e.g. Joyce 1990). The link is used as a tool to break open the meaning of the source page, rather than to restrict or specify. Meaning appears to be constantly in motion, always slipping through the hands of the user, allegedly creating the urge to reengage in reading or engage in rereading. In *253*, however, links have a meaning that can be explicated. There is a connection between the source and the target node and this is semantically (mostly metonymically) embodied by the link. Very often this results in thematic subwebs connecting inline anchors. In a way, *253* does what it mocks in the first announcement, it "uses the miracle of information technology to ensure that you can follow the main themes and relationships that link the text" (ad1.htm). Some of these subwebs will be dealt with in the thematic analysis at the end of this article!

Some pages can only be properly understood in connection with thematically related pages. Debbie DeNussi, an American filmmaker, is lost in London. She is expected at the Royal Pharmaceutical Society, but the instructions she was given turn out to be incomplete. Without following the right link, it is nearly impossible for the user to find out that the woman sitting next to her is the receptionist waiting for her. Inline thematic links can play a major role in the generation of meaning. "Reconsidering the material for print publication has led Ryman to a startling discovery about the power of links and hypertext on which the web is based: They change the meaning of the work" (Grossman 1997). Consequently, when the user has read all the words, it is very likely that even on a physical level she has not read the entire novel, because some links have not been pursued. Moreover, since the browser colors all links to visited pages purple, it is very likely that the user approaches each page from only one direction, missing out on all the alternative entrances and hidden meanings.

253 *as a narrative*

In the previous section we have seen how the hypertext organization of *253* is based on the layout of a London underground Bakerloo line train. Passengers are grouped by cars and cars can be reached through the journey planner or directly from the first page. The structure of a hypertext does not only have technical or practical consequences for the user; it also influences what we could call narrative syntax, the way in which the story itself is laid out. In this section, we will look at how the geographical metaphor is incorporated in the narrative through a frame story. Next, we will investigate how the movement through the hypertextual space, the paths followed by the user, can influence both semantics and user experience. Finally, we will look at how focalization and fragmentation enforce one another in order to create a multiplicity of views on one scene.

In the subtitle, *253* is announced as *a story about the London underground in seven cars and a crash*. This is at once the structure of the fiction and the frame story. By juxtaposing the crash with the seven cars (both in the structure and the title), the crash seems to be trivialized giving the whole a sense of cynicism, of black humor. Moreover, it could be a playful reference to the creation myth. The author is acting like a deity, creating a train in seven cars, like God created the universe in seven days. The crash could then be seen as an omen, a reflection on judgment day. In view of the fact that the novel is situated within a train (symbol of progress) driving toward its end, links the God theme to the theme of modernity (cf. infra). One motive behind the morbid frame could be a feeling of impotence by the author. "253 happens on January 11th 1995, which is the day I learned my best friend was dying of AIDS" (why.htm).

Like in most print examples, the frame story of *253* is used as a syntactic device to facilitate structuring. There is no teleological tension-building and the climax (the crash) is already announced in the title and repeated in the introduction. Moreover, most individual pages lack tension building towards a climax, although some groups of linked pages do, e.g. the Gary Collier and Amanda Stinton incident (cf. supra). There is, however, some sort of an eternally postponed climax in the reading act itself. *253* is written in such a way that it induces a sort of passionate greed to know what comes next when the user pursues a link to a character that is involved in a situation previously described by an antagonist or fellow victim. As a reader you want to know how the other characters experience the same situation or conflict. Will they add elements to it? Contradict it? Simply dismiss it? In other words, it is the reader's own curiosity that prevents her from losing interest. Finally, there are examples of subnarratives where the frame story plays an even more important role. Paul Launcey is deeply depressed. He has serious debts and he is thinking on how he could commit suicide and make it look like an accident so that his family would benefit from the insurance. In the final phrase the narrator exerts his godly power. "The train sweeps him on towards the Elephant" (101.htm), where he will die in the crash.

Hypertext structure, mediated through narrative, has a direct influence on the reading process. In *253* the user can approach most nodes from different angles, following a different reading path, seeing everything through other characters' eyes. On the one hand, there is a certain independence between hypertext and narrative syntax. A similar narrative constellation can be represented in different formats (hypertext or linear). On the other hand, the way in which the story is laid out pofoundly influences meaning production and the constitution of narrative elements within the reader's head. Furthermore, by truly juxtaposing passengers' viewpoints (same number of words, same structure for each character) a number of different versions of situations are sketched. It is the reader's task to assemble these views and build her own picture.

As a case study, we will look at car number three where a performance of *Mind the Gap* is taking place, a play consisting of different acts performed on the train. A paying audience follows the theater group through the underground. Passenger 96, Geoff Ryman, is an amateur actor taking part in the performance. When he stands up to look at one of the underground maps in the train, a woman takes his place and without looking he sits down on her. Ryman, horror-stricken, stands up, hits his head on the rail and sits down on another passenger who is the fellow actor on whom he should have sat the first time. Interestingly, this same scene is described by different groups of passengers, some of whom are attending the performance, others not.

Lawrens Timmins, an American professor who has paid to watch *Mind the Gap*, thinks it is great fun (94.htm). Doris McPherson, the woman on whom Ryman accidentally sat takes it well. "'Any time you want to sit on my knee, feel free', she says to the young man" (95.htm). Rafael da Cunha, believes wholeheartedly what he sees unfold before his eyes. "He [the actor, jvl] doesn't notice when an old lady sits down in his seat. The idiot sits down on top of her. Some dumb American by the look of him. Rafael doubles up" (85.htm). Vitrola Feldmoue however, a famous actress, is more critical-minded. "(...) when his second victim, the fake City gent, scuttled across to the seat next to hers, it all began to look rehearsed. She smelled it: failed actor, poncing about for free. 'This is a put on, isn't it?'" (88.htm). Ben Bevis finally, the actor on whom Ryman was to sit, feels jealous. "To go ahead and sit on a real passenger instead of the plant was brilliant! And then to sit down on Ben anyway and make it look convincing!" (87.htm).

By piecing together the fragments of the passengers' accounts, a clearer image of the scene slowly emerges. The woman Ryman sits on is no longer a poor victim, but an independent, assertive old lady who deliberately snaps up Ryman's seat. According to Ben Bevis the original routine was supposed to be performed using a plant. He finds Ryman's improvisation brilliant, but the more experienced actor, Vitrola Feldmoue, immediately feels that the scene is rehearsed. Then two policemen arrive and ask for a license for the performance. Officer Bert Harris hates both his job and the people he is confronted with. "Now we got some berk bothering people for a bunch of fun-lovers. An old dear is getting off. 'Do you want to make a complaint?' Bert asks her. She just grins at him and gets off. She's gaga. Put her in a home" (98.htm). James Bartlett is embarrassed by his bully colleague. He gets off the train and interrogates an American student who was watching the performance. "Bert fancies her, so he keeps her talking" (91.htm). The girl is more cunning however. "Sara thinks: I'm young, I'm sexy, I'll just do this until you get bored and let us go" (92.htm).

Depending on which nodes of the web have been read, an entirely different picture is drawn. In linear fiction, this effect would largely be lost simply due to the fact that every reader follows the same reading path. Even if the meaning generation differs and different readers pick up different bits and pieces from the narration, a similar effect can only be arrived at in multi-linear or non-linear fiction. Hypertext could, in this way, be an excellent tool both to investigate reading behavior and to substantiate heuristic theory.

Every passenger page is divided into three sections. The first section is a seemingly objective account of what the passenger looks like, titled "Outward appearance." It pretends to be an objective account, mostly using direct definition (Rimmon-Kenan 1983, 59), of what a fellow passenger would see. Ben Bevis is described as "an advertising executive from some 1950s sitcom" (87.htm) whereas in fact he is a professional comedian. In other words, the narrator is feigning ignorance of the true occupation of Bevis and only reveals his identity in the following section called "Inside information." He focalizes the description through the eyes of a fictional observer in the train. Sometimes Ryman mocks this format. Sam Cruza's outward appearance is described as that of a New York taxi driver. In the second section, the omniscient narrator confirms this as if being a New York taxi driver is a distinguishing feature, as if someone could look like a New York taxi driver, but not like one from Chicago.

In other cases, the use of the format is more crucial. Jason Luveridge is described as "Late teens, black male. Slumped in green baggy track suit, American sports jacket and baseball cap" (36.htm). This description very much conforms to the stereotype of lower class black boy, but it clashes with Jason's true story. His mother saved enough money to send one of her children to St. Paul's School. The narrator explains that Jason is academically gifted and he will be writing a thesis on Charles Dickens. However, the other children at home make fun of him when he wants to hear classical music or watch Panorama. Therefore, "[h]is clothes are camouflage. He expects to wear camouflage all his life."

The third section of every passenger page is called "What he/she is doing or thinking." This is where most intrigue and action is developed, where the different stories and situations are laid out. Very often, this is done through the eyes of the passenger the current page is devoted to. Many events are focalized without the intervention of the omniscient narrator, creating the multiple possible interpretations we have briefly touched upon in the *Mind the Gap* case study. Direct speech provides a way of presenting this seemingly unmediated type of narrative. However, very often the narrator remains present through free indirect speech. "Bert arrested him for indecent exposure, which was the best joke of all. Animals. Even animals don't do it in toilets" (98.htm). In one case, the difference between these two types of communication is flagrant. Georgina Bullen can no longer stand the smell of her neighbouring passenger Kevin Potter who suspects nothing. When describing the scene focalized through the eyes of Georgina, it is minimized. "She explodes and says perhaps too much... something about burnt tyres" (40.htm). When the scene is focalized through the eyes of Kevin Potter, it is significantly more drastic and probably more accurately described. "To his horror the woman sitting next to him erupts, jowls quivering. 'This is unbearable', she announces. 'Can't you use a deodorant? You smell like a bonfire of old rubber tyres!'" (40.htm).

Thematic analysis

In the previous sections we have described how *253* is a textual experiment using structured hypertext, and how multi-linearity in narrative design at the same time opens and closes doors to storytelling. But *253* is more than just a literary experiment using a new medium. Modernity is not only part of the structural, but also of the thematical network. The course of the underground train could be seen as a metaphor for mankind moving towards its end. Significantly, Ryman seems to have ambiguous feelings about progress, pointing at both the danger and the idiocy of certain developments in modern times. Deirdre Hidderley is an art student who believes all modern art like Kandinsky, Bacon, Auerbach is a result of synaesthesia (33.htm). Julie Gluck, a gallery owner, is fed up with the London art scene. "Friends stage openings, drink cheap wine, skittishly look for critics who never arrive, and then leave the pictures on the walls for two weeks. (...) Nobody bothers to steal them. It's called art" (236.htm).

Sometimes the past is described with an undertone of melancholy. Before the Tubes, everything used to be better, more humane. "[Anthea Dobbs] looks at the silent people around her and remembers the tube strike of 1989. Everyone walked to work. It was summer, and London was suddenly a festival of people" (217.htm). Anthea is saved: "She suddenly yearns to be out on the streets and abruptly decides to walk to the Elephant from Waterloo." It is the divine hand of the author that seems to interfere here, saving Anthea by and with her utopian vision of the past. Sometimes the narrator shows himself to be downright conservative. Beryl Barber is reading a book on English History. The book is described by one very meaningful phrase: "It is divided into units not chapters" (86.htm). Calling chapters units apparently does not improve the quality of the work. "[Beryl Barber] finds it deeply boring." Modernity is depicted as a two-edged sword. On the one hand, progress provides new opportunities, on the other it does not automatically mean improvement.

Typical problems of modernity like racism and migration are developed in several interlinked nodes forming thematic subwebs. Keith Olewaio likes his work. He is a young African who came to England to be a minicab driver. He has decided to stay although he experiences great difficulties finding his way around London. "Under the laughter, he is becoming coldly determined. I am fool, he thinks, until I learn" (9.htm). Toby Swiswe, his fellow cab-owner has been in Britain longer. "Mr Swiswe remembers how Britain first looked to him, calm and orderly if slightly deadened" (10.htm). He told his colleague he had an accident. In reality, their car has been smashed by white racist youths. "They shouted at him; he did not understand. They gestured at him to come out. The lights were red, he could not escape. They started kicking his car, and wrenching off the antennae. 'Stay out of it, you black bastard!'" Toby feels guilty, his cousin had told him to stay out of Hammersmith.

253's structural framework does not allow for in depth treatment of complex problems. The limit on the length of the pages and the multi-linear structure make it difficult to develop arguments. However, it is very easy to have many different characters with different backgrounds approach one problem from their perspective. Linked to the Cab-incident described above, there is the story of John Kennedy, a young bookmaker who saw a Pakistani couple being stoned by white youths. John is shocked; the kids look just like him. "The girl wept in her boyfriend's arms. 'We shouldn't have been there', she sobbed. (...) She had a Snoopy badge on her coat" (122.htm). When John tells the story at work, his colleagues laugh, John does not understand.

There is never any real inquiry into the hows and whats of the problem of racism. Instead, the user is offered a whole range of descriptions of how different people in society experience the problem. These loose fragments form a decentered structure providing the reader with a patchwork of ideas and thoughts. It is up to the user to assemble the bits and pieces into an image of how racism is experienced by its victims as well as its offenders. No one group within society is blamed for what goes wrong. Africans experience racism in London, and a Turkish girl growing up in England is harassed in Istanbul because of her Western clothing and hair (119.htm). The problem is not dramatized. Anup Agnihotri, half Indian and half Ugandan, has lived in England for 19 years and people still cannot understand his accent. He is described as a "happy, outgoing, capable man" (116.htm). He likes being in England. "How do they do so well here?" In the final sentences, the narrator poses a very important question. "How much further does he need to go? Can he go?" (116.htm). The answer is left open.

Sometimes the question of modernity is directly linked to ethnic issues. Michael Lipkin is an accountant for Pall Mall Oil. He feels out of his time being a Jew who studies the scriptures. Michael believes modernity is dangerous for tradition. "Sage, thoughtful Jews like himself allowed themselves to be herded into camps" (64.htm). He feels threatened by the younger generations and describes them with dislike. "New Jews are big, bronzed, crew-cutted soldiers who enjoy cunnilingus." Catherine, one of these new Jews feels betrayed by tradition. When she was 17, her synagogue organized a production of *Fiddler on the Roof*. Because she was not pretty, she had to handle the lights. "The hall was to be in darkness, until the first line. Catherine couldn't find the right switches. The hero entered a baldly lit temporary hall, and said, "Let there be light." Catherine plunged the hall into darkness" (248.htm). Her conclusion is the same as Michael's, tradition seems to be opposed to modernity. "What had been meant to be beautiful had become terrifying: there was no light, not from God. Why else would so many of her people have been killed?"

Louisa Balbrough happily embraces modern rational thinking. She has discovered a letter from her father to her mother in which he tells her he has another son, Peter Wolffe. In this way, Louisa finds out she is in love with her half brother. She decides to stay with him and folds the letter away. "I'm 50; there can be no children, there are no Gods to enrage" (224.htm). Religion itself does not seem to be the problem; it is extremism. Indirectly, the train accident is caused by Islamic fundamentalism because the driver did not sleep enough due to a late night discussion on the subject. For Gurdev Dhollin, all religions are personal. He is dismayed by the invention of Hindu fundamentalism. "Where does this come from? The term Hindu refers to geography not belief" (168.htm).

Strangely enough, there is some sort of an ending to *253*. The very last passenger in the train is called Anne Frank. She has been wandering through Europe for 50 years without finding peace. She symbolizes both the wandering Jew and the memory of what modernity did to mankind during the Second World War. Anne wants to make the people happy one more time before they die, just like the people on their way to Auschwitz. She stands up and starts to sing *Is that all there is?*, a 1950's hit by Peggy Lee. The composers, Stoller and Lieber, based it on the story *Disillusionment* by Thomas Mann. It deals with a boy who sees a house burn down and thinks: is that all there is? Ever since then, life has been a series of disappointments. All the great experiences left him with a feeling of "is that all?" It is a story about general disillusionment, not a miscarriage in small matters, but disappointment about life itself and what it has in store. Only when the protagonist sees the sea for the first time, he feels no disappointment. A sea without a horizon leaves him with a tremendous craving for freedom. One day, he believes, death will come and it will be just one more disappointment (Higgins 1997).

In Peggy Lee's song, the part about the sea is left out, laying more emphasis on the morbid ending. Most of the verse in the song is spoken rather than sung. The refrain goes as follows.

> Is that all there is?
> Is that all there is?
> If that's all there is, my friend,
> Then let's keep dancing,
> If that's all
> there
> is.

If even destruction is only destruction and death is only death, why be afraid of what is coming? "One must be calm and laugh" (179.htm). The people in the train start to dance like Peggy Lee. Only Harold Pottluk does not dance. He is a market researcher for the London Underground. He is described as having "listed people on carriages by age, gender and racial background" (252.htm). Anne asks him to dance, but he refuses. Even more people join in and at Lambeth North, the last stop before the end of the line, Anne makes sure everyone but Harold and herself gets off the train. Harold dies in the crash. Anne does not. She cannot die. She pulls herself out of the wreckage and takes the list from Harold's bloodied hand. It is a list of people who do not use the underground, they are described as the "useful people who will survive: the unemployed, the sick, the retired and elderly..." (end7.htm). Anne leaves the tunnel; she will be the living memory of what modernity has done to her people. "Anne knows such lists. She knows all the names, the millions of names."

Conclusion

253 bears characteristics of both a novel and a theatrical play. It is written to be read, but dramatic irony, fragmentation and locality give it a theatrical feel. The Internet is more than a deliverer in that it influences both the form of the novel and the reading act. By molding the narrative space into a very rigid hypertextual structure, *253* succeeds in creating a navigational network reducing the cognitive overhead often experienced in hypertext narrative. Linking plays an extremely important role, not just because it changes the sequence according to which the nodes are read, but also because it changes the meaning itself. The textual space from which meaning is to be deduced is three- instead of two-dimensional. Both hypertextual and narrative syntax are grafted upon a frame story, i.e. an underground train about to crash, in which decentering, fragmentation and focalization steer the reader through an ingenious type of hypertext story, providing a unique view on modern society through modern media.

Works cited

Berners-Lee Tim (2000). *Frequently Asked Questions* <http://www.w3.org/People/Berners-Lee/FAQ.html>.
Gibson, William (1984). *Neuromancer*. New York: Ace Book.
Grossman, Wendy (1997). *Geoff Ryman's Web novel, "253", peers into the heads of a Tube train-ful of characters as they hurtle toward an uncertain fate*. <http://www.salonmagazine.com/march97/21st/london970320.html>.
Higgins, George V. (1997). <http://www2.hawaii.edu/~lady/snapshots/peggy-lee.html>.
Joyce, Michael (1990). *Afternoon, A Story*. Electronic text. Watertown, PA: Eastgate, 1990.
Keep, Christopher & McLaughlin, Tim & Parmar, Robin (1995). *The Electronic Labyrinth*, <http://jefferson.village.virginia.edu/elab/hfl0098.html>.

Landow, George P. (1997). *Hypertext 2.0: The convergence of Contemporary Critical Theory and Technology*. Baltimore (Md.): Johns Hopkins University Press.
Lewis, Antony (2000). *WordWeb 1.62*. <http://www.x-word.com/thesaurus/>.
Matthews, Harry & Brotchie, Alastair (1998). *Oulipo Compendium*. Atlas Press: London.
Murray, Janet H. (1997). *Hamlet on the Holodeck: The Future of Narrative in Cyberspace*. New York: The Free Press.
Nelson, Theodore Holm (1993 [1981]) *Literary Machines*. Sausalito, CA: Mindful Press.
Rimmon-Kenan, Shlomith (1983). *Narrative Fiction: Contemporary Poetics*. London, New York: Routledge.
Ryman, Geoff (1996). *253 or Tube Theatre, a novel for the Internet about London Underground in seven cars and a crash*. <http://www.ryman-novel.com>.
— (1998). *253, the journey of 253 lifetimes: the print remix*. London: Flamingo.
Tolva, John (1995). *The Heresy of Hypertext: Fear and Anxiety in the Late Age of Print*. <http://www.mindspring.com/~jntolva/heresy.html>.
Van Looy, Jan (1999). *Authoring as Architecture: Toward a Hyperfiction Poetics*. Leuven: K.U.L., MA-thesis.
Voss, Wilf (1998). *The Young Professionals Group: Newsletter: 253. An interview with Geoff Ryman, author of 253*. <http://www.spikemagazine.com/0398_253.htm>.
Wachowski, Larry & Wachowski, Andy (1999). *The Matrix*. Warner Bros.
Winson, Leonie (2000?). "A Reactive Interview with Geoff Ryman author of 253". <http://www.innotts.co.uk/~leo/hyper/253.htm>.

III
Cybertext

Requiem for a Reader?
A Semiotic Approach to Reader and Text in Electronic Literature

Jack Post
(University of Maastricht)

One thing is for sure, by placing the adjective 'electronic' before 'literature', the literary text finds itself in the midst of the rapidly evolving field of new communication technologies of the 20th century, such as radio, television, computer, holography, cellular phones and the Internet. In their attempt to define 'electronic literature', Eric Vos and Jan Baetens state that the integration of the characteristics and possibilities of electronic information systems in the textuality of the literary work, leads to the introduction of *temporality* and *changeability* in the inscription of the literary text (Baetens & Vos 1999: 439). Specific properties distinguish electronic literature radically from traditional printed literature, and lead to a different sequentiality of the text (hypertext), to a convergence of different media such as text, moving image and sound (multimediality), or to a dynamical manipulation of the visual dimension (moving, morphing and mutation) of text. Speaking about electronic literature is thus speaking about substantial changes in the appearance and treatment of text, and about a different experience of literature itself. That the convergence of media leads to a blurring of boundaries between genres and media, becomes clear when one browses through Web sites devoted to electronic literature. Some texts published on those sites belong to the traditional literary corpus, others are more difficult to categorize, they look like movies, animations or illustrated soundtracks. The appearance and experience of these electronic texts is different and changes the status of the reader. Do we still read electronic texts and what are we as 'readers' of an electronic text supposed to do: read, write, look, listen, or embark upon the labyrinth of a hypertext? These questions are not new or exclusively related to 'electronic text', but the intervention of technology into the literary text is, as stated by Baetens & Vos, a radical prerequisite for the mere definition of electronic literature.[1]

Should one characterize a Web site which uses text artistically in combination with media technology, and which not explicitly pretends to be literature, as a form of electronic literature? To give a preliminary answer to this complex question, the present article focuses on the role of the text and the reader, thereby leaving aside intriguing questions about use of (photographic) images, sound, voice and music. The Web site Darren Aronofsky created for his film *Requiem for a dream* will serve as a case study.

Convergence of media: book, film, trailer, teaser, Web site.

In recent years, cinema and the promotion of film, have become important issues on the Web. Studios not only distribute trailers on the Web, they put up complete Web sites to promote their films. At first those sites were just 'press kits' with a trailer, some pictures of the actors, and information about 'the making of the film'. The success of *The Blair Witch Project* and the decisive role of its Web site in the marketing strategy made clear that sites can be an important extension and enhancement of film. Another example is the Web site Darren Aronofsky created for his innovative black and white film 'Pi'.[2] This film, about a mathematician who is obsessed with computers and numerical patterns and who thinks he can calculate the course of the stock market, offers extensive information and lessons on the topics covered in the movie, such as Cabala, numerology, the game Go and the stock market. Sean Gullette, actor in the film and designer of the site, states that this Web site is the medium par excellence to experience the world like the main character in the film: "The movie is about paranoia and cabala, and since the Internet is a paranoid and intertwined medium, it's well-suited to convey those ideas" (Cavanaugh 1998).

For his second film, *Requiem for a dream*, Aronofsky created an award-winning Web site using Macromedia Flash.[3] Flash, a Web-technology to create vector-based animations and navigation interfaces, enables Aronofsky to evoke the paranoid experience and agonies of addiction, the topic of the film. The film is based on Hubert Selby's novel by the same name. It tells the parallel stories of four characters struggling with addiction: the lonely widow Sara Goldfarb, her son Harry Goldfarb, his girlfriend Marion

---

[1] For a discussion on literature and digital media, see Ryan 1998.
[2] See <http://www.pithemovie.com>
[3] The *Requiem for a dream* web-site won the first prize in the category 'interactivity' at the Flash Film Festival in London (27 November 2000).

and his friend Tyrone. Sara lives in a Brooklyn-apartment and is addicted to chocolates and television shows. After a rather vague phone call, she thinks she has won a place in her favorite television show. In order to fit into the beautiful red dress she wore in happier times, she has to lose 20 pounds. Inspired by infomercials on TV, she decides to put herself on a diet and starts taking diet pills. Harry, Marion and Tyrone use drugs from time to time, but do not consider themselves 'drug-addicts'. Marion wants to be a fashion designer and dreams of opening her own boutique with Harry. They hope to finance their dream by selling drugs. In search of the great drug deal they dream of, Harry and Tyrone are constantly on the road, looking for that 'pound of pure, uncut heroin' that will set them free. As time goes by, Sara is taking more and more pills, and gradually Harry, Marion and Tyrone start to use more and more of the heroin they meant to sell. They are all on the downward slope and their physical and psychological situation deteriorates. They are all spiraling deeper and deeper into addiction, the drugs are taking over their lives and their warm and sunny dreams turn into a dark, hellish nightmare.

In an interview with Jory Farr, Selby stresses that his book is not about 'junkies', but about 'the great American dream': "about what happens when you pursue an illusion and turn your back on a true vision of what life is really about' and that 'eventually, the pain in indulging the drugs becomes greater than the pain you're trying to avoid. Then you're really caught in a terrible trap" (Farr 2000). To drag the reader into this nightmarish world of obsessions, cravings and delusions, Selby uses a visual and graphic style, with its own rhythm, spelling and typography. To depict the hallucinating world of addiction, with its excitement of being high and deceptions of being down, and its thrills of the ever repeating rituals, Aronofsky employs a visual and surreal cinematographic style in his film.

The viewing of the film is a harrowing and hallucinating experience because the editing pace of the film is very fast (2000 cuts instead of the normal 600 to 700), the film is full of repetitions, images of submarine and surveillance cameras, and a whole range of optical effects from slow and fast motion, split screens, dissolves and fades, to digitally manipulated images. Selby himself was very impressed by the cinematic devices Aronofsky used to get inside the characters of his book (Farr 2000).

Like the film, the Web site of *Requiem for a dream* is an experience onto itself, and should be considered an independent complement to the film. The concept of the site, which uses images, text and sounds taken from the film, is specially adapted to the medium of the Internet. Instead of a flashy billboard for the film, Aronofsky and Florian Schmitt, the designer of the site, strove to design a site which reflects the tone of the film and offers an experience onto itself. According to Schmitt the site "mirrors the film, but we were looking for metaphors to use on the Web. (...) What is addiction on the Web? Gambling? Infomercials? We wanted to convey that' (Elder 2000). Thus the remark of a reviewer that 'Visitors to Artisan's Web site for its film *Requiem for a Dream* won't find the names of stars, a plot synopsis or even a release date. Instead, they'll find an impossible-to-navigate site, in which users lose control and spiral into chaos" (Elder 2000), should not be interpreted as a shortcoming or even worse as a disqualification of the site. On the contrary!

Trapped in Flash

The site opens with a splash-screen showing the title of the film, and then suddenly it seems to be hacked by a commercial Web site, TappyTibbons.com.[4] The visitor is forced to follow the directions given by the Tappy Tibbon site. Tappy Tibbon, known from TV, makes you a winner in your familial, mental, physical or financial life: "We got a winner," You're winner," "Lean and clean in 30 days," "Make a fortune." The site keeps the visitor in a state of suspense, giving the impression that the computer is crashing, or that the Internet connection is broken. All this is part of the aesthetics of the site which, according to Schmitt, deconstructs what most Web sites are and underlines the chaos of the film. This impression of an ever increasing instability, and an emotional and psychological state of addiction, which the site conveys, is a metaphor for addiction on the Internet, and functions as an equivalent of the visual style of the film. Schmitt uses Flash to create an experience of 'losing control' and of 'being trapped' in the Web site. Aronofsky: "You think every once in a while it's making more sense, but slowly it just gets out of hand, and you end up in hell" (Elder 2000).

Macromedia's Flash has become very popular because it enables the designer to use animations, full-screen transitions, anti-aliased typography and Mpeg3 sound in a Web site, without heavy download times. Because Flash makes virtually 'everything' possible, it became not only the privileged tool for the avant-garde and arty Web sites (such as Kioken or Soulbath),[5] but also for the creation of sites for big companies like Sony, Disney, Nike or IBM.[6] Around Flash an ever-growing community of Web-designers emerged who call themselves 'flash-artists'. Lev Manovich

---

[4] Florian Schmitt, the designer of the Web site got an email from a visitor, warning him that the site had been hacked by TappyTibbons.com.
[5] See <http://www.kioken.com> and <http://www.soulbath.com>
[6] See <http://www.macromedia.com/showcase>

speaks of them as 'generation flash', a new generation which is "no longer interested in 'media critique', which preoccupied media artists of the last two decades; instead it is engaged in software critique. (...) The result is the new modernism of data visualizations, vector nets, pixel-thin grids and arrows: Bauhaus in the service of information design" (Manovich 2002). But the widespread use of Flash did not remain without critique. It became a thorn in the flesh of usability experts and interface designers who worry about the decreasing usability of Flash-sites. Their critique on Flash is severe, as the titles of their articles indicate: "Flash is evil," "A Cancer on the Web called Flash" or "Flash: 99% Bad" (MacGregor 2000; Nielsen 2000; Ragus 2000). Their critique is mainly aimed at the disabling of the most common Web-navigation: "Flash sites render useless the browser's Back button and address bar, and make bookmarking pages inside a Flash site impossible. Printing Flash pages from your browser does not work, nor does intra-page keyword searching. Finally, Flash sites eliminate HTML links' visited and unvisited colors, and that color-changing feature is the Web's single most important navigational cue" (Ragus 2000). You can also say that these negative characteristics of Flash are exactly the reason that big companies build their sites with Flash. Flash gives them some control over the Web-surfers: "Companies create unique user experiences around their products and services, involve their audience into on-line quizzes and games, try to keep users on their sites and – more importantly – make them come back. www.nikefootball.com is an example of an immersive and addictive user experience" (Zmoelnig 2000). In other words, Flash creates immersive environments which encapsulate and 'stick' users to the site, giving them the sense of 'real' experiences.

Immersion and addiction

Schmitt intentionally brought the immersive qualities of Flash, especially the possibility to capture the visitor in the site into action. After the fake hijacking of the Web site, the order seems to be restored when a second splash screen appears with the title of the film. But gradually the page turns white and nothing happens, the disquiet visitor starts moving the cursor impatiently over the page, and discovers that it hides a puzzle. Moving the cursor starts music, and uncovers pieces of an image. Gradually a kaleidoscopic image surfaces, in which we recognize the figures of Harry and Marion, lying next to each other. The figures turn out to be 'hot spots' which, when clicked, turn red and start a sequence with Harry (and Tyrone), Marion or Sara.

128 HYPERTEXT READINGS

All sequences consist of three successive parts, each indicated by the name of a season: summer, fall and winter. The 'story' starts 'in media res'. At the moment the characters think their dreams will eventually come true, Spring with all its promises has already passed. The succession of seasons indicates the passage of time, and more particularly the inevitable downward spiral caused by drug addiction taking over. The Web site evokes this worsening of the situation and the growing apart of the characters by means of an increasing chaos in image and sound and by giving the visitor the sense of losing control over the navigation of the site. The navigation is unreliable: you never know if clicking will bring you where you want to go: Web pages suddenly turn into HTML-code, sound disappears or changes into hissing, the cursor moves strangely or is multiplied, etc. The further the visitor goes into the site, the more the feeling of being lost and trapped increases. At the end of this mesmerizing and terrifying experience, the visitor returns to the puzzle page and may start his or her journey through the site all over again. But the next experience will probably be totally different. One gets the impression that the site is never fully explored and seems to recreate "the terrible trap of addiction" Selby speaks of (Farr 2000).

Flash and text

Since Flash is based on vector graphics technology it is able to handle text in a flexible way. With Flash, text can be animated, scaled and morphed smoothly without jagged edges and fuzziness. Many Flash-sites make use of text, because Flash makes text so malleable and gives the site an 'artistic' or 'poetic' look. The somewhat static and abstract images of *Requiem for a dream* are photographic collages combined with straight lines and sharp-edged colored shapes. This gives the site a particular look, which reminds one of the typographic experiments of Russian Constructivism and Bauhaus. This look may partly be due to (or inspired by) Flash-technology itself, which is based on mathematical equations, curves and lines.[7] The text is projected in, along, through and over the images projecting meaning onto them.[8]

One of the most touching and impressive passages in the whole site is a telephone-scene between Harry and Marion, the 'last call' which signals the end of their relationship. This sequence is almost entirely built up of text: pieces of dialogue, isolated words, sentences, whole paragraphs, HTML-code and ASCII-art. The sequence starts with the caption 'Fall'. We hear the beeps of a telephone call, which are visualized on screen by little signs, and suddenly different visual representations appear on the screen: abstract shapes of crabbed handwriting, a vertical line which divides the image plane in two halves, an agglomerate of text with the words 'requiem' and 'dream', and finally, the silhouettes of Marion and Harry. When the whole is settled down, the silhouettes of Harry and Marion, divided by a dark plane and superimposed with text fragments, are filled with photographic detail. The silhouettes of Harry and Marion turn red when they start to speak, and the words of their conversation appear over the image:

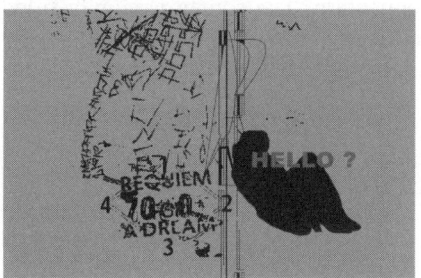 

During the sequence described above, fragments of HTML-code flicker over the scene, and for a short moment we see the image of a skull made up of ASCII-text emerge, and at certain points the whole is interrupted by computer error messages.

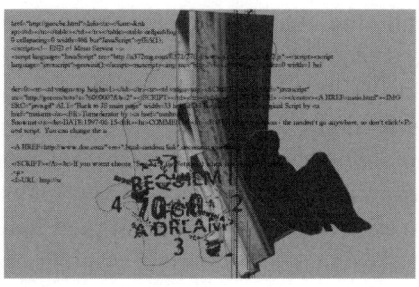 

---

[7] See also Manovich on the modernist aesthetics of Flash-sites (2002)
[8] Roland Barthes states that text anchors the meaning of images (Barthes 1982).

 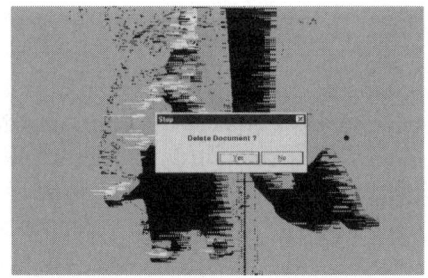

The sequence takes place in about 5 seconds, which means that the pace is very fast, and that actions take place on different levels and simultaneously[9]. At the end of the telephone scene, Harry and Marion are on the verge of despair, because they know their parting is definite. Their silhouettes are now filled with ASCII-signs, and decay bit by bit. The words of their conversation remain on the screen, just like the fragments of HTML-code. Finally, the sound of the telephone connection deteriorates until it is broken and we only hear the sound of a broken telephone connection. The screen is slowly filled with a black zone, which accentuates the words: "I'm really sorry, Marion."

 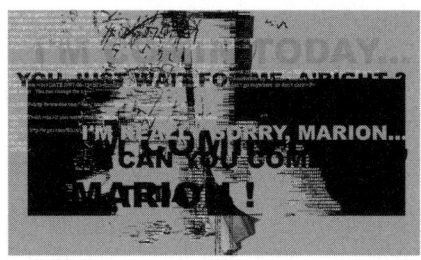

The other sequences follow more or less the same pattern. For instance, in the Fall sequence for Sara, which is located in Sara's kitchen, we go through a similar disintegration. Gradually the image is superimposed with fragments of text, in separate windows, as plain black text lines, red lines of HTML-code, remains of a disintegrating Web page of TappyTibbon.com and slogans which materialize Sara's obsessions.

It is obvious that the description and analysis of these sequences is not exhaustive; it is only meant to give an impression of the role text plays in the conception of the *Requiem for a dream* site. It may be argued that

---

[9] Hence, *Requiem for a dream* is a complex site that is difficult to describe and analyze. Now that the problems of film-analysis and citation are more or less solved by the technology of analog video, we are anew confronted with problems concerning the analysis of digital (moving) images, for instance the analysis and citation of protected Flash-files or streaming video.

 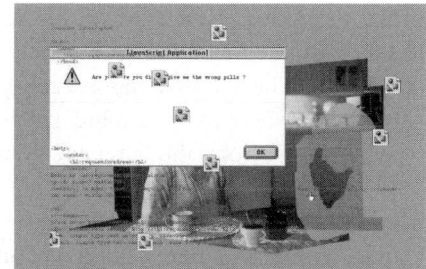
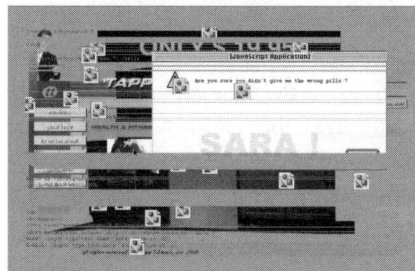 

this site is not simply a marketing tool of the studio, but a consciously designed form of Web critique aimed at provoking the visitor.

Semiotics of the visual text

In 1979 Julien Algirdas Greimas and Joseph Courtès published *Semiotics and Language. An Analytical Dictionary* and a few years later Greimas published a little brochure called 'Figurative Semiotics and the Semiotics of the Plastic Arts' (Greimas 1984; 1989 English translation). Greimas and Courtès state: "writing is the manifestation of a natural language by means of a signifier the substance of which is visual and graphic (or pictographic) in nature" (375). They explicitly refer to the materiality of the signifier, which is the "external plane of language (...) manifested by its perceptible qualities" (300) and enables us to classify the different semiotic systems, and to differentiate between sensorial orders of the signifiers, such as photography and typography. But Greimas and Courtès state that this sort of classification does not inform us about the way the signifier itself is organized and articulated. Typography, spoken language or photography cannot adequately be defined by their respective signifiers as their specificity must be sought in the "articulation mode of the form of the signifier" (300). Greimas and Courtès thus differentiate between substance (materiality) and form (system) of the signifier.

From a semiotic point of view, the substance or materiality of the signifier is to be considered as a variable which manifests the invariant semiotic system (or form). The English language system can be manifested by different substances, such as a graphic substance (writing) or a phonic substance (speaking), whereby the language system itself does not change.

In his article on 'Figurative semiotics' (1989), Greimas gives some indications on how to use semiotics to analyze visual aspects of writing. Greimas defines writing as a *planar structure* and therefore as the object of visual semiotics,[10] which include not only pictorial, graphic or photographic representations but also various types of writing. Recognizing markings on a surface as writing implies that we consider them as signifying wholes or signifying systems which justifies the intervention of semiotic theory (629). In the first occurrences of text in the Web site of *Requiem for a dream* for instance, the markings we identified as 'crabbed handwriting', we are able to recognize for instance 'E', 'N', the words 'Koko' or 'AND', and something which looks like a handwritten line, but we are not really capable to decipher the whole:

The second form of writing we encounter on the site is markings which are undoubtedly alphabetic and numeric signs: ciphers, 'Requiem for a dream' or dialog lines:

Because we perceive and recognize the material traces as the material manifestations of a linguistic signifier, we consider a planar object like a Web site as a semiotic process which realizes the virtualities of the semiotic

---

[10] He states that visual semiotics "is often no more than a catalogue of our perplexities and incorrect facts" (Greimas 1989).

system of the English language. Greimas speaks about the projection of a 'reading grid', which allows us to interpret the markings as the figure-letters of a graphematic organization.

The third form of writing we encountered in the Web site are strings of HTML-code, which prove that the figure-letters of the English language can be used by formal languages, such as systems of logical representation or mathematical notation. They make use of the same 'alphabet', but the internal organization of the letters is indifferent to them: "Whereas writing as a system depends on the oppositions between its various graphic features ('round', 'hooked', and so on), formal languages consider the letters they use to be discriminatory (630). Therefore the signifier of a formal language possesses no graphic system like the writing system, it's just a catalogue of discrete symbols or concepts, that can be represented in many ways.

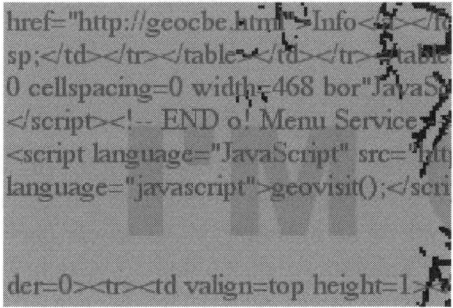

The last form of text we hit upon is the alphabet used as material for figurative images (i.e. ASCII-art), like the silhouette of Marion and the skull:

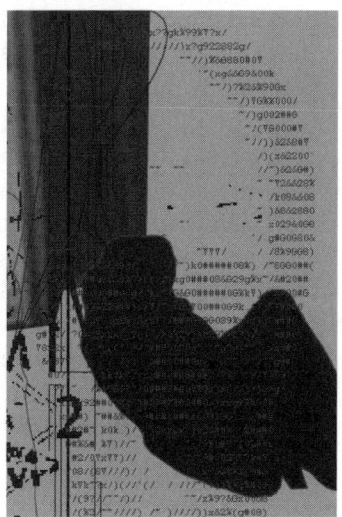

Ergo, reading markings on a planar surface is constructing signifiers by projecting 'reading grids' onto the graphic substance. This means that the same visual substance (the Web page) can be segmented in different ways and with a view to a certain kind of reading: we use a conceptual grid to interpret visual markings as the symbols of a formal language (HTML-code), a graphematic grid to articulate the substance into figures-letters of a linguistic language, an iconic figurative reading grid to recognize the markings as objects of the world (the skull, the silhouettes of Harry and Marion, Sara's kitchen) and an abstract figurative reading grid to identify the markings as abstract figures (the abstract shapes between Harry and Marion, or the written scribblings). The same materiality of the Web page is thus subject to segmentation into different substances, which are articulated by different forms or systems. This means that we might speak of different texts, different readings and different readers.

The Web site as a poetical text

In her discussion of the experimental typography of Marinetti, Drucker (1994) detects two simultaneously occurring processes of signification within a single work: "The meaning of the words derived as much from their position, their relation to each other as visual elements and their movement as a series of marks across the sheet, as from their semantic value" (137). This demonstrates that the typographical page can be read in at least two ways: as written language which produces linguistic meanings, and as visual language (the manipulated signifier of the written language) which produces supplemental significations. Greimas classifies the categories Drucker mentions (139) such as form, position, relative direction and orientation within the page, into topological categories (upper versus lower, left versus right) and plastic categories (colors and form).[11] These categories inform the plastic form of the signifier. And like Drucker, Greimas relates these (plastic) categories of the signifier, to (semantic) categories of the signified. Drucker correlates for instance the plastic categories, which are always correlations between opposite terms, such as 'large' versus 'small' of the signifier of the majuscule, with the semantic categories 'more important' versus 'less important' of the signified, or 'order' versus 'disorder' of a typographic page with the elements 'noise' versus 'silence' of the signified (44, 138). Greimas emphasizes that these elements, since they are categories of the form and not categories of the substance,

---

[11] With the 'chromatic categories' referring to color and 'eidetic categories' referring to form.

form a semiotic system.¹² In the case of typography for instance, this semiotic system engrafts itself onto the signifiers of the primary (linguistic) language and causes a supplementary or secondary segmentation. Greimas considers this secondary segmentation of the typographic page as a plastic language (system) which is superimposed on a first language (system) which itself is limited to its primary functionality. The secondary (plastic) language detaches the signifiers of the primary language to transform them into signifiers of its own with an autonomous organization. Between the model Drucker proposes to analyze the avant-garde experimental typography and the theoretical model of the plastic semiotics of Greimas, many common grounds may be found. Both speak about a process of secondary segmentation of the linguistic signifier and characterize this as a 'subversion' of the hitherto functional typography. A subversion which causes multiple readings of the same textual object and turns it into an aesthetic object with a life of its own (Drucker 1994: 139; Greimas 1989: 647).¹³ Greimas goes even further and speaks about a 'poetic reading' and the birth of a 'poetic language': "It shows how a functional object, used in social communication, can be transformed into an "aesthetic object"…" (647).

Reading or viewing texts

The text of a Web site like *Requiem for a dream* can be considered an 'aesthetic object' and even as 'poetic text'. One can even go as far as Greimas, and state that the existence of an autonomous poetic language or semiotics "with all its structural organization and modes of signification" abolishes the "conventionally established boundaries that separate different domains of manifestation" (647), and conclude that if the substance of the signifier becomes of secondary importance, the 'poetry' of the text is of primary importance. What is at stake, is the poetical structure, the secondary poetical organization of the text, and the different, separated, convergent or maybe even conflicting readings or readers they mobilize. We are of course not dealing with 'real' readings or 'real' readers, but with abstract actants or processes of semiotic enunciation. To distinguish different modes of typographic enunciation, Drucker (1994) introduces the opposition between marked and unmarked

---

[12] Greimas characterizes this kind of semiotic system as "semisymbolic semiotics" (Greimas, 1989: 646; Greimas & Courtés 1979: p. 290).
[13] When the secondary visual language becomes dominant we speak of 'language art', when the linguistic language remains dominant, we speak of 'visual poetry'.

texts.[14] The uniform pages of the bibles Gutenberg printed, are to be regarded as the archetypes of unmarked texts: "he printed bibles with their perfectly uniform gray pages, their uninterrupted blocks of text, without headings or subheadings or any distraction beyond the occasional initial letter. (...) text in which the words on the page 'appear to speak themselves' without the visible intervention of author or printer" (95). The tradition of the unmarked text became the standard for the literary work which, in order to allow the reader a smooth reading, avoids any visual interference. The marked text is on the contrary a product of the 'subversion' or 'deconstruction' of the conventions of the unmarked text. Marked texts place the reader explicitly in relation to the various levels of linguistic and graphic enunciation of the text. Therefore, the reader of an experimental Web site such as *Requiem for a dream*, is not only reading linguistic texts, but also looking at the text, listening to sound and touching the mouse button.

This tension between reading and looking is not entirely new, but its significance has increased with the recent convergence of media and genres. The typographic experiments of the Futurist and Dadaist avant-garde poets Drucker analyzes for instance are inextricably bound up with the rapid development of production and reproduction technologies in the late 19th and early 20th century. Commercial designers emphasized the visual properties of the printed page, to shock and seduce potential customers. The avant-garde poets, who experimented with various typefaces and different reading zones on one page, with colors, images etc., introduced eye-catching typographical tactics into the literary domain. With visual codes, they aggressively violated the conventions of the literary texts, which were eventually codified by Russian Constructivists, the German Bauhaus and the Dutch Stijl who established 'graphic design' as a professional discipline. Làszlò Moholy-Nagy, one of the advocates of the 'New Typography', sought to integrate word and image, typography and photography into what he named the 'typophoto' (Moholy-Nagy 1991: 39). According to Moholy-Nagy 'typophoto', or the new visual literature, is better suited for the modern dimensions of the industrial world with its communication technologies, than the traditional forms of printing. With its "simultaneous experience of vision and communication' it enables direct visual contact with the masses and demands an active participation of the reader who more than ever becomes a viewer and participant" (75).

---

[14] Richard Lanham introduces a similar distinction, when he states that the transparent design of traditional printing wants the gaze to look through the design, and that the self-conscious and opaque typography of the avant-garde artists wants the gaze to look *at* the surface of the page (Lanham 1993: 43).

The same convergence of reader and viewer can be observed in the 'electronic poetry' produced by the Brazilian poet Eduardo Kac.[15] Kac achieved fame for his holopoetry and holopoems, new forms of electronic literature he invented in 1983 to overcome the shortcomings of the two-dimensionality and linearity of the printed page. Holopoems are textual structures in three-dimensional holographic space which continually change shape, color or position. It is difficult to decide if the reader of a holopoem is a 'reader', a 'viewer' or 'participant'. In his theoretical works, Kac constantly shifts between reading/reader and viewer/viewing: "engagement on the part of the reader or viewer," "the viewer looks for words," "the reader has never seen" or "the viewer has to read" (Kac 1993). The holopoems introduce changeability and temporality into the literary text, which not only has consequences for the text but also for the reader:

> By textual instability I mean precisely that condition according to which a holographic text does not preserve a single visual structure in time as it is read by the viewer, producing different and transitory verbal configurations in response to the beholder's perceptual exploration (Kac 1997).

Requiem for a reader?

Should we speak about a viewer, a reader, a visitor or a participant in an electronic text? It depends on which definition we provide for 'reader'. The notion of unproblematic reader of transparent, unmarked literary text is useless vis-à-vis most electronic texts. Electronic texts are for the greater part marked texts,[16] composed out of two of more different signifiers (visual, formal, linguistic or musical), and each of these asks for the projection of a different 'reading grid', produces its own reader. Consequently, an electronic text has multiple readers who are never, from a semiotic point of view, the 'real' receivers or readers of the text, nor are they defined by the visual (viewer), linguistic (reader) or musical (listener) substance of the signifier. These readers (or enunciatees, Greimas & Courtés 1982: 105) are the implicit actantial roles of the artistic or poetic enunciation, positions which enable the reading, deciphering or decoding of the different artistic or poetic languages in actu. Hence,

---

[15] It becomes increasingly difficult to talk about writing in the case of electronic literature.
[16] Which texts are considered marked is bound to historical time. Marked text will be codified and will establish in its turn a new dominant convention. The new 'reader' of electronic literature will be one of the models to interact with the new cultural products of the 'electronic and digital revolution'. For a short semiotic definition of the term 'marked', see Fontanille 2001 and Greimas & Courtés 1982.

the role of the reader is a complex and changeable construction, just like the notion of 'text'.[17]

Text is to be considered as a non-analyzed entity, as the material and concrete manifestation that has to be analyzed. Text is the totality of the material which presents itself to the senses of an embodied reader: the graphic, phonic, visual substance of the expression. Text can be syncretic, that is to say, it can consist of a combination of different substances: visual and graphematic for instance. Although most scholars use text as a synonym for discourse, it should be opposed to discourse.[18]

Discourse has to be distinguished from text because it is defined as the semiotic activity of attributing meaning to textual structures. Discourse is to be considered as the enunciation in action or the enunciative praxis by which the 'reader' (enunciatee) reconstructs the meaning of the directly perceivable appearances of the text. This 'reader' searches for values and meanings that transcend the given materiality of the text. And in this reconstruction of the meaning of a text, the readings, but particularly the processes of totalizing rereading, are of crucial importance. In contrast to the explorative reading of the textual structures, the construction of the discourse always presupposes a totalizing rereading of the text. In other words, all different (converging, diverging or conflicting) readings should be brought together in order to be converted into a meaningful whole. Text and discourse are thus two different ways of approaching the same textual object.

In conclusion, we can say that the convergence of media is able to produce very multifaceted electronic texts, such as the *Requiem for a dream* Web site, which are experienced by their readers as highly marked. The 'reader' is to be considered as a bundle of various 'readings' corresponding with the different semiotic systems or forms actualized in a syncretic text. In the analysis of the Web site of *Requiem for a dream* we reconstructed several of these semiotic systems: the system of the English language, the system of the formal language HTML, a reading grid for the objects in the natural world and a reading grid of plastic forms such as abstract shapes, colors and movements. Thus far we do not dispose of 'a set of habits' to construct a totalizing (re)reading of this kind of text. At the same time we consider these texts as 'aesthetic objects' with very complex signifiers which do not allow a simple 'totalizing reading'. Flash technology enabled the designers of the *Requiem for a Dream* Web site to play with different semiotic systems in such a way that the visitor is not only confronted with a mixture of different textual systems, but is also forced to look at and

---

[17] We have to keep in mind that these notions, such as 'enunciatee', 'text' and 'discourse' are entities of analysis and are not to be found in reality.
[18] For a discussion of the notion text in relation to electronic literature, see Fontanille 1999.

listen to the text, or even to touch it. This play with different activities and competencies blocks the possibility of a total (re)reading and creates a strong experience of disorientation and addiction. In any case, the advent of electronic literature not only shifts the boundaries of what we consider to be literature; it definitively ends the dream of the unproblematic reader and makes a 'Requiem for a reader' more than appropriate.

Works cited

Barthes, R. (1982). Le message photographique. In *L'obvie et l'obtus. Essais critiques III; Tel Quel* (9–24). Paris: Éditions du Seuil.
Cavanaugh, T. (1998). Hollywood Squared. Pithemovie.com puts Hollywood's uninspired Web Sites to shame. *Salon*.
Drucker, J. (1994). *Visible Word. Experimental Typography and Modern Art, 1909-1923*. Chicago: University of Chicago Press.
Elder, Robert K. (Oct. 22, 2000). *Navigation Tools. Moviemakers Seek New Ways to Use the Net as Yet Another Way to Promote Their Films*. Retrieved Feb. 12, 2000, from <http://www.chicagotribune.com/leisure/artsandentertainment/printedition/article/0,2669,SAV-0010220306,FF.html>
Farr, J. (2000). Savage Vision. *The Dallas Morning News*.
Fontanille, J. (1999). Préface. In A. Vuillemin & M. Lenoble (Eds.), *Littérature, Informatique, Lecture. De la lecture assistée par ordinateur à la lecture interactive* (I–VIII). Limoges: Pulim.
Fontanille, J. (2001). Enveloppes, prothèses et empreintes: Le corps postmoderne. *Protée, 28*(3), 101–110.
Greimas, Algirdas J. (1984). Sémiotique figurative et sémiotique plastique. *Actes sémiotiques - Documents, Vi*(60), 5–24.
Greimas, Algirdas J. (1989). Figurative Semiotics and the Semiotics of the Plastic Arts. *New Literary History, 20*(3), 627–650.
Greimas, Algirdas J., & Courtès, J. (1979). *Dictionnaire raisonné de la théorie du langage*. Paris: Hachette.
Greimas, Algirdas J., & Courtès, J. (1982). *Semiotics and Language. An Analytical Dictionary*. Bloomington: Indiana University Press.
Kac, E. (1993). Holopoetry, Hypertext, Hyperpoetry. In Tung H. Jeong (Ed.), *Holographic Imaging and Materials (Proc. SPIE 2043)* (72–81). Bellingham, WA: SPIE.
Kac, E. (1997). Key Concepts of Holopoetry. *Electronic Book Review* 14(1).
Lanham, Richard A. (1993). Digital Rhetoric and the Digital Arts. In Richard A. Lanham (Ed.), *The Electronic Word. Democracy, Technology, and the Arts* (30–52). Chicago [etc.]: University of Chicago Press.
MacGregor, C. (2000, jun 1, 2000). *A Cancer on the Web called Flash*. Retrieved March 16, 2001, from <http://www.flazoom.com/news/cancer_06012000.shtml>.
Manovich, L. (2002). *Generation Flash 1-3*. Retrieved 10/04/ - 02/052002, 2002, from <http://www.nettime.org>
Moholy Nagy, L. (1991). The New Typography. In R. Kostelanetz (Ed.), *Moholy-Nagy. An Anthology* (75–76). New York: Da Capo Press.

Nielsen, J. (2000). *Flash: 99% Bad*. Retrieved March 13, 2001, from <http://www.useit.com/alertbox/20001029.html>.

Ragus, D. (2000). *Flash is Evil*. Retrieved March 15, 2001, from <http://www.dack.com/web/flash_evil.html>.

Ryan, M.-L. (1998). *Cyberspace Textuality. Computer Technology and Literary theory*. Bloomington, Ind., [etc.]: Indiana University Press.

Zmoelnig, C. (2000). *Skip Intro. An Aesthetic and economic analysis of Macromedia's Flash technology (MA Hypermedia Studies 1999/2000)*. Retrieved March 16, 2001, from <http://www.sensomatic.com/chz/skipintro/>

The Narrative of an Interface: Rethinking Hypertext Theory by Face-ing Design Questions

Paul A. Harris
(Loyola Marymount University)

The Interface to a Print Essay about Hypertext

Writing a scholarly essay about hypertext and new media to be published in print takes one out of familiar places and roles. The digital medium as both the 'subject' and 'object' of writing infiltrates the process; the scene of writing being the screen transforms the nature of the practice one pursues. This essay began as an investigation of the way in which the primacy of the database as an organizing principle of text is transforming the nature of narrative. In essence, the database serves as the interface to narrative – it instantiates a skeletal mannikin within which the body-text is draped. But what results is not a static form that contains content – rather, a recursive dynamic evolves in which Web sites and hypermedia works embed narrative elements (lexia) within a linked structure, the design principles of which then come to shape and, more, become an integral part of the narrative content – which in turn may effect reconceptions in the design as the work unfolds. As text lurches vertiginously out of its familiar print contexts, context and content morph, become inseparable enantiomorphs; suddenly, as context becomes an x factor, content has n possibilities; context is just whatever tent there is for text to nestle into – hopefully snugly rather than smugly. With these notions firmly implanted in my head, I began to set about assembling the elements of the essay. But something funny happened on the way to this forum for ideas – the same recursions I was aware of in what I was staring at began ripple through my work: the dynamics and practices I was describing became inseparable from the text I was writing. What began as a study of the interface to narrative became a narrative of the interface, and its ever-changing faces which find expression in various textual guises.

The experience I invoke here is no doubt common to many of us embarking on the enterprise of writing about hypertext within the parameters of critical theory and literary criticism. And the tempting move to make next is an adaptive, mimetic one – to write for print as if one were writing in a hypertext environment, or at least to claim, with a tone of somewhat lame regret, that the essay is better suited for the 'other' medium, the one outside the covers of the book the reader will hold when they read the precious words one writes. But I found that behind the discomforts that come from attempting to stake stable claims on shifting grounds there emerged two basic issues. The first is a larger one, which encompasses writing in whatever medium happens to be at hand – the question of how language and our relation to and use of it is changing as we upload our minds into the new media ecology. The second is what tools prove useful when one seeks to mine a rich vein amid the rush that envelops the world(s) where text circulates these days. Often I feel as if the golden opportunities that surround me on the U.S'.s West Coast are eluding me, because I am using an outdated toolkit to tap into the information stream. Rather than enter into what could quickly become a preponderant meditation on these probably unmanageable questions, I have chosen to address them in a hands-on spirit that favors performativity over description, experiment over explanation.

Attacked from a pragmatic standpoint, these issues take on a more definite shape. The fuzzy problem of how language and our use of it is changing, when brought into brightly pixeled focus, becomes a question of nomenclature – what are the words we use when we describe and engage in writing in the new media ecologies? What informs the simple choices we make about what to call things, and how do these choices inflect or already express our position within the game? The trick here is to avoid renaming new tools according to old ones – "electronic book" is tantamount to saying "horseless carriage." Yet we must also remain cognizant of the irreducible duality or duplicity of a landscape where electronic and print media cohabit, still codependents who get in each other's way as much as they synergize new relationships. Katherine Hayles recently proposed that media art works that combine text, image, and animation, and overlay several kinds of writing, be called "multicourse." Hayles explains that "multicourse can be understood as a neologism for 'multiple discourses' but [it] also alludes to the multiple reading pathways generated by links and computational combinations." The term marks a spot where electronic and print media interest, in that "'multicourse' acknowledges both of electronic literature's parents."

From a further standpoint, "multicourse" also evokes a fundamental characteristic of an emerging sensibility towards language – all discourse units are inherently multiplicities. It's a bit slippery to pin down (of course!), but we examine words, books, songs, TV shows, plays, movies in a meta-mind's eye – we're attuned to what lurks behind things. Sampling, spin-offs, riffs, scratching, remixing, splicing, cloning, cutting and pasting, randomizing...we have tools that can capture and reconfigure material in ways that mimic our brain's wetware's proficiencies at slipping from one slope of thought to another. It's with a combination of suspicion and delight that we walk around feeling that any word might be another, any one chunk of text might link you to something completely different, any given song can be sampled. Elsewhere I've discussed this as part of process of "virtualization" operative in many spheres: in the noosphere, where Deleuze's "virtual" plane defines a mode of thought; the textual sphere, where fixed texts become actualized versions of a network of virtual potentialities; the mediasphere, where the virus called language gets moved from the stable, weighty world of words to the virtual reality-tinged pixel multiverse (ebr10).

Faced with this process, one immediately broaches the second issue I raise, that of adequate tools. As a critic writing about the relations between database and narrative, I consulted both print journals and online 'zines to ferret out examples of literary and/or critical happenings on the Web. I was acting as a literary critic boldly seeking out new worlds where no one had gone before – part of the strange space one gets into, where one wishes to hold to the value of lasting contribution to a critical canon even as one treks about looking for undiscovered stars who will raise one's own star in the process of writing about them. In shifty times, one tricks oneself into rendering oneself obsolete – without successfully becoming two selves. Seeking to suture the gap between critically distanced observer and the speed, novelty and urgency that permeates the changing literary landscape, I began to adopt behaviors consistent with what I was studying – I opened multiple programs and windows, downloaded Web writings, started to edit them into suggestive configurations. But I still felt disengaged from the material, in that I was compiling examples that fell under categories, rather than engaging the real issues that compelled the project in the first place – namely, the interface between database and narrative, in both literal and literary terms.

But then, poking around in the obscure corners of my hard disk, I stumbled onto the perfect tool for the task at hand. In reading 'old' email from some friends, I unwittingly opened Eudora's box, and out popped the very embodiment, the perfectly exemplary example of what I had been mulling over all along: an exchange between several people about redesigning the interface for an online literary journal. This object proved perfect for sifting through several pressing matters in the multicourse world – the interface to a journal which itself is an interface between print and electronic media is a scene where database meets narrative, where nomenclature becomes volatile, and where theoretical and historical questions become situated, hands-on problems to be solved. Following the loopy lines along which these discussions unfold – messages pile up and scatter in several directions, and then someone compiles the list of salient issues at hand – I found that one participant had pithily put a finger on just the things that I had begun to notice and think about, in the process of sifting through databases, interfaces, Web sites, and media experimentations:

> These issues of database construction, interface design and context, publication as active event, navigational cues, visual metaphors, environmental logic, reader-response "picture theory" etc., are crucial. So my first suggestion is that we archive these group emails as they evolve.

Here, then, were the terms I needed, here were the airy things I had been implicitly sounding out, but for which I had no names. Thankfully, there *was* what amounted to an archive, and most of it was intact, and available for use.

The Context

In 1997, a group of texts replicated themselves by splitting: essays and reviews about writing and new media were simultaneously published in the *American Book Review* and went up online, in the *electronic book review*. The progenitor of the project, Joe Tabbi, threw out these opening words: "To introduce an electronic book review, in the very medium that is reducing book technology to a museum piece, is to confront some of the more persistent cultural contradictions of the past few decades.... For those writers who are committed to working in the new electronic environments, such a 'review' might better be named a 'retrospective', a mere scholarly commemoration of a phenomenon that is passing" (Tabbi, "Review"). In retrospect, it was completely apt that the review was spawned as a dual print/electronic creature. The journal has continued to investigate work in and concerned with both media – Web-based writers are regular contributors; new print fiction and criticism continue to get reviewed; experiments with how to create intersections are favored. Tabbi's words have proved a bit premature, since the print world continues to thrive, and more often than not, writers work and publish in both print and electronic outlets. We remain wired into the "cultural contradictions" Tabbi refers to, but they seem less contradictory. And as of the date I'm writing – lo, these many years later – the *electronic book review* has accumulated a history. By Web standards, it is a venerable presence, having amassed an archive of eleven issues.

The site itself (http://www.altx.com/ebr) has 'naturally' evolved a great deal in its long life. The first issue was simply a white screen with a banner with the journal name at the top; the format was essentially a hyperlinked table of contents that sent you to the articles (http://www.altx.com/ebr/ebr1/ebr1.htm). The interface mimicked what you found when you open a lit-crit journal, and *Ebr*'s mission statement read like a journal taking tentative first steps on a new planet: "ebr is an electronic book review, an online forum allowing critical writers to present their work on the Internet. We are committed to reviewing (literally, seeing again) every aspect of book culture – fiction, poetry, criticism, and the arts – in the context of emerging media. At the same time, ebr is a review of electronic books, promoting translations and transformations from print to screen, and covering literary work that can only be read in electronic formats." The effort to import the seriousness and value of the *literary* into the weirdness of the *electronic* is palpable here – and utterly understandable, given the reluctance at the time to credit online journals with being genuine in any larger professional sense.

Typeface

Fast forward to the present – which of course will be outdated by the time these words see print. *Ebr* has a totally different look; graphics are sometimes designed specifically for issue themes, and the interface is sharp, and sets a distinctive tone and mood – against a gridded black background that has both an industrial-textile look and a floating quality, the screen has four linked categories/headings:

These coinages manage to combine a slightly inviting opacity with a somewhat self-explanatory character. Tabbi says that the terms "were chosen and named for a certain conception of hypertext INFOrmation processing, involving some fluctuation between VIEWing, POSTing, and READing" (email). Such allusions are likely lost on screeners, but the aptness of the terms for what they open onto when clicked indicates the way that nomenclature gets entrained by context – old words function in new ways, new words come to seem natural. In place of the plain text missions statement from the first issue, a block of text is embedded in a tag on the screen:

146   HYPERTEXT READINGS

> promoting print/screen transformations
> and weaving new modes of critical writing
> into the web

The longwinded high-lit mission statement about being "committed to" various things has been replaced by a breezy riff predicated on electronic publi/shing/city "promoting" work. The tag's retro look gives it its cool feel – the faded typewriter letters a throwback to the medium being left behind, the faded look itself made possible by pixel potentiality, the letters' presence in the Web exemplifying the imbrication of the two media they call on others to explore.

One curious result of these changes worth noting is that they leave the journal's name a bit unwieldly. What was christened at the moment of a Web-based spin-off from a respected print journal now had become something else entirely. Ewan Branda, an *ebr* Programming Consultant, conveys his feeling that when he tells someone "what the initials [*ebr*] 'stand for' (interesting phrase, that) I feel compelled to immediately add 'it's not just reviews'. In fact, all three words in the title seem to me to overdetermine the journal's content in ways that seem quite reductive in view of *ebr*'s current editorial praxis. So I don't think *ebr* 'stands for' electronic book reviews at all." What the journal does in fact not only stand for, but even encourage, became part of the discussion when the interface entered the arena.

The Interface Review Board

In the summer of 2000, the *ebr* interface came up for review. It was subjected to a number of criticisms that questioned the work it was doing, and wondered what directions it might take in the future. The composition of the review board tells us a lot about the multicourse world:

> From *ebr*:
> - Joe Tabbi, Editor
> - Anne Burdick, Design Editor & Site Designer
> - Ewan Branda, Programming Consultant
> - Sophie Dobrigkeit, Design Contributor
>
> Other faces:
> - Rob Wittig, formerly in In.S.Omnia, now director of literary studio *Tank20*
> - Mark Amerika, founder of alt-x and famed e-author
> - Jan Baetens, academician committed to new media studies
>
> Plus a virtual face that never appears – a position that needed to be filled:

- I'm looking for an experienced DHTML programmer to build the front end for the new *electronic book review* interface. This is a high-profile site that is currently under reconstruction. The project promises to be quite provocative in terms of both publishing models and interface design.

We need to find someone capable of programming the front end of a site with:
- dynamic layouts
- interactivity
- some JavaScript
- custom pull-down menus

This collection of individual talents needed to think through an interface for a literary journal illustrates the separation that persists between the skills needed to traverse and help create the multicourse terrain. Some day one person will embrace all these roles without thinking about them being distinctly different; operating from some more malleable platform, they will spin out potential changes with the flick of a wrist.

A historical parallel comes to mind from chaos theory, the development of which was, like multicourse, computer-driven. Thomas Weissert recounts a seminal scene in chaos theory history as follows:

In the Spring of 1952, the MANIAC-I computing machine came on line at Los Alamos. One of the first digital computers, it filled a large room, used vast arrays of large, hot, glowing vacuum tubes for computation, and processed box after box of permanently inscribed, single-command, disposable, punched cards. That summer, in a professional configuration foreshadowing the disciplinary alliance of the future, physicist Enrico Fermi, computer scientist John Pasta, and mathematician Stanislaw Ulam, gathered together to discuss the computation potential presented by the speed, accuracy, and relentless automation of these new electronic marvels. (Weissert 9)

The discussion among people with varied expertise that it took to formulate a problem and subject it to exploration with a computer has been eclipsed by changes in machines and training. Weissert begins his book by describing his visit with a "dynamicist," who sits at his workstation and runs a model that simulates chaotic behaviors – "by immersing his senses, sight and touch, the dynamicist was climbing into phase space and taking it for a ride" (viii). Is this person doing computer science, mathematics or physics? Well, it depends.

I don't mean to imply that the literary sphere is lagging half a century behind science in any way, but the integration of skills in the multicourse world seems a long way off still. This slowness emerges from many converging factors and habits: the universities remaining structured to channel minds into particular pockets; the fear that the values and canon of Literature and Books will evaporate in e-space; the social separation between the literary sphere and the tech-sphere where programmers live, and so on. From this vantage point, there is something quite fitting about the simple fact that the discussion of an interface for a Web site about interfaces between print and electronic literatures became an interface where several differently skilled people gathered to address several key issues in the multicourse/verse today. The "cultural contradictions" we are facing will ultimately get negotiated in just this way – as the needs and wishes of literary minds rub elbows with the practical possibilities delineated by designers and programmers.

Enter the Interface

From the outset, the exchange about the *ebr* interface makes clear that its form is integral to the journal's content. Consequently, the interface is not only a structural but an expressive tool; or, put differently, the lines between database structure and *ebr*'s textual contents become effaced in the concerns that emerge around its composition and function. The interface crystallizes one of the central functions served by the journal: namely, that it is itself a sort of database about or interface to writings in print and on the Web. Tabbi imagines that "along with discussions of issues raised by the essays and hypertexts and art installations in *ebr*, the journal should offer an annotated Web surf, with perhaps a different guest surfer every month, whose commentary might extend over several days." Here, the key components to a Web surf guide, a sort of *Michelin* that would never tire, are reader participation and constantly changing contents that would keep pace with the speed with which additions are made to the Web-writing world.

The larger goal in redesigning the interface was clearly to incorporate the single most crucial aspect of electronic writing: its dynamic character. As more and more motion and change get coded into Web sites, the simple pointing and clicking that had freed literary hypertext from the fixed confines of print has come to seem but a clumsy attempt to open text to a dynamic world. The burden of the discussion revolved around how the interface could itself become an ever-shifting, active screen presence, and how it could change the roles and decisions of editors, contributors, and readers in the process.

Face Types

Initially, Joe Tabbi imagined the interface as a logical extension of the existing presentation of the journal. As a literary critic, he focuses on the etymological and epistemological associations between text and weaving:

> The new design will take the textile metaphor and conceive of each individual essay as a thread that interweaves with other essays and themes. The interface is a fabric comprised of these threads – the visual patterning is a result of the ways in which they are organized – their affiliations, connections, and the hierarchy of filtering concerns.

Here, the hypertextual nature of the journal remains rooted in the fractal nature of hypertext – meaning a relation where all parts reflect the whole in some way, and a whole (the interface as synecdoche for the journal in its archival entirety) reflects all the parts. Tabbi later expresses the wish that the interface serve as a "map (and archive) in which a representation of every single essay is visible at all times – each essay's appearance is a representation of its position within the site as a whole (in relation to other units, themes, time, user interests...)." The primary concern here might be termed formal – how the form of the interface expresses the fractal nature of the journal.

The approach from a design and site editor comes in more programmatic terms, as it were. When Anne Burdick responds, she thinks in terms of what the people involved actually do, and how the interface will change as the journal takes in new content.

> What we want to create is a dynamic database structure that operates according to the following procedure: Simply, as the editor/s edit, each decision has a "rippling" effect throughout the site (map), as it is represented through the interface. As each essay is added to the database, the editor installs the essay, creates links within its body, then answers a few questions in terms of the essay's affiliation with other parts of the journal (mostly with other essays or themes). Dynamically, the representation of the new essay finds its place within the weave.

Worth noting here is the emphasis on the "dynamic" elements at play in the process of formatting and uploading essays into the site. The database is called "dynamic" because editors would change its configuration in ways commensurate with new contributions. The database per se remains static though, in that it would be a single fixed screen, even if it differed with each issue.

The next step in the conceiving the interface's design was to see it as a cybernetic entity, an algorithm that would allow the interface to modify itself according to procedures programmed into it. A lower-maintenance, less editor-controlled interface:

> building a machine that will make updating simple and in some ways a "natural" part of the editing process. With each update/editorial gesture (and perhaps reader's gestures), the machine will generate an interface which, according to its assigned logic and parameters, could reflect emerging patterns of use, interest, and editorial intentions.

The interface becomes part of a feedback loop that includes editors and "perhaps" readers. The idea that it "could reflect emerging patterns" in site composition and navigation interestingly mixes in a sense that beyond a rule-governed, top-down designed entity, the interface will be part of a journal whose developmental logic becomes one of bottom-up 'emergence'. Anne Burdick seems to note that the interface is being referred to as an entity with some sort of integrity or presence when she realizes that "I've been speaking of it as a machine, but it's actually an application."

Soon after this, the interface as mechanical tool all but disappears. As notions of how the interface could change configurations with usage multiply, the machine comes to be seen as a self-organizing entity unto itself. The more dynamic the interface, the more life – and even lives – it has.

> The idea of creating a "machine" that responds to the community and reconfigures the interface in such a way that the community can then respond-to-the-response exhibited visually (and thus cause further metamorphosis), is stimulating beyond words (for me). That is, can we both map "each essay's appearance as a representation of its position within the site as a whole" *and* map the community's live engagement with those appearances?

The interface does not merely shift its configuration as a screener navigates the site. Rather, it "undergoes further metamorphosis." This is "stimulating beyond words" – an intriguingly literal usage of an idiom, in that it alludes to the extra-textual components in the interface that would be central to its formation and effect. Finally, these attributions of life to the machine arrive when the interface is imagined as reacting in 'real time' to users, now themselves seen as a whole-larger-than parts "community."

As the internal exchange between *ebr* editor and designers began to broach more and more issues that clearly spoke to larger questions within the 'community', external voices were brought in. Tabbi created a mailing list and subscribed people to it, encouraging a much wider forum for the ideas being bandied about. At this point, a virtual interface – a potential one waiting to happen – gave rise to an actual interface, a common context for many people to share thoughts. With the rhetorical panache of the seasoned Web-writer and theorizer, Mark Amerika offered this summary of the discussion to that point:

> Hybrid practices cause shifting momentums. As the energies of the distributed team of cultural producers collide and mix, the interface is subject to metamorphosis. Sometimes this happens because the machine applies itself. Sometimes this happens because the reader applies herself. Sometimes this happens because the writer/artist applies herself. Not to mention the environment these hybrid-applications exist in.
>
> All of this should somehow manifest itself visually and, ideally, automatically.
>
> The database becomes a kind of reliable narrator.

Amerika's comments have a dual effect: first, they create a narrative about the interface, where it is spoken of as a sort of protagonist caught up in a convergence of several forces and influences. The interface becomes a sort of chameleon figure, changing as each source of control enters the scene; then it suddenly takes on an agency of its own when it becomes automated. On a different level, the interface becomes an author-ity figure in relation to the journal/site it frames. The database cast as "reliable narrator" makes the site an ongoing story whose trajectories and relations are determined by the stabilizing or anchoring presence of the interface.

In functional terms, the interface as narrator means that it tells what is happening in the arena of action where users interact with the site. Amerika offers an example of such an interface: he describes an installation by Auriea Harvey, a Web artist and graphic designer, called "ANANATOMY": "Her interface," Amerika writes, "allows all of the visitors to her site know how many other visitors are there in live-time by metaphorically re-presenting each user as an animated sperm moving in toward the egg that is centered on the screen." The interface, it seems, becomes "reliable" to the extent that it is "automatic." It registers what transpires on the site as it happens; reliability also is synonymous with real-time usage.

One or Many Faces?

Both postmodern fiction and hypertext writing did much to enervate and at times explode the idea of a single, governing narrative authority. In place of a narrator or clear narrating presence, the narrative function became distributed. The same shift occurs in this little story of an interface. The interface as "reliable narrator" comes under fire from Rob Wittig, a writer who champions multiple inputs, media, and storylines in his work. Counter to Amerika's emphasis on a "purely automatic" interface, Wittig insists that "A purely autopoietic algorithmic machine would be boring. Many programmers have made it a Holy Grail to devise a nest of algorithms to... automatically... link new pieces of design-writing together in a meaningful way. The results are sometimes interesting, but most often dull." Extrapolating from this position, Ewan Banda proposes that the "interface might even begin to reorganize the connections and groupings in ways other than those intended by the editors. The visible relationships would reflect the intersection of editorial interests and reader interests." The 'self'-organizing principle of the interface suddenly becomes a function of several 'selves', with no one in absolute control. Distributed autopoiesis, perhaps, rather than a single-organism or structured process.

The interface so reconceived becomes a cyborg. Wittig offers his counsel: "try that [purely automated interface], if it interests you, but don't leave ALL the linking functions to the machine. Have machine-linked views AND Human-DJ-Linked views" The result is a recreational scene where the screen becomes comparable to a DJ's workstation – where several turntables and programmed tracks can be played off and into each other. Wittig sees the interface as "a perfect place for human hands on the keyboard. Like on a synthesizer/sampler keyboard. Play the links like a musical instrument. Joe's personal Re-Mix. Joe's Academic Re-Mix. Anne's textile Re-Mix. Guest Re-Mixes. Mix-It Yourself. People are great at making connections. Playful and unpredictable. Brains are built for playing with connections." And so the screener becomes a re-mixer, and the interface no long narrates the site, but becomes caught up in a continuously re-tangled loop between screener, editor, and archive.

Saving Face(s)

As soon as discussions synergize and begin to project information configurations whose very nature is embedded in the emerging media, the recursive loop bends us back on our own reflections. How are current pathways going to be rewired in the new mode of thought and practice? Once the interface came ungrounded, it had suddenly become a potential playground where *ebr* could be continually recreated. As a result, the journal would lose its 'identity', in a way: Burdick observes that "The 'dynamic' component of the interface – as we are imagining it – is the fact that there is no fixed single representation of *ebr* as a whole." However, the journal remains constrained by its obligations to the publishing domain in which it was launched and continues to persist. The unmoored, multiple personality interface, which would present a different face each visit, presented certain dilemmas for the editorial side of the discussion – specifically, how the identities of contributors and articles would be preserved and presented in this new format.

Having lost its original purpose or design as the database equivalent of a table of contents, the interface had to be rethought all over again. Burdick brings the discussion back to page one, as it were, asking, "Which organizational logics / categorical subdivisions are interesting to us? Which territories do we wish to map?" First, there were the seemingly essential or given aspects of contributions, held over from the print journal paradigm:

- date of publication
- author
- subject matter
- theme

But then the interface and its environment present other possibilities for how to organize and present the information, as well as how to register the usage of the site by others. The other categories up for discussion include:

- number of links within an essay
- most "popular" essays or themes
- most recently visited essays or themes
- connections (reader movement) made between essays not linked
- connections (reader movement) made following editorially-determined paths/links
- editorial-based connections (links within essays, visited or not)

In essence, the interface becomes a workshop or laboratory where the journal's Web-based setting renders the archived contents a virtual configuration that can be navigated in any number of ways. Very quickly though, one sees that the seemingly 'pure' 'potential' of unlimited possible links and routes through the site become shaped and constrained by different factors. Top-down editorial control over links between pieces already deflects multi-coursing readers along certain courses. Bottom-up reader created links would seem to decentralize control, and registering the most popular themes or most visited pieces would seem to be a way to give the people what they want.

At the same time though, it is precisely this sort of practice that quickly feeds the strong and starves the weak – any piece that gets more play at the outset is likely to be what subsequent readers click on as well. 'Popularity' is not a negative feedback, always renegotiated in a democratic fashion sort of process; it is a passive consumer pattern of following trends. The sheer access and amount of information available make it daunting enough to try to keep up with the literary profession, new work in print and electronic media, let alone cool new stuff appearing on the Web every hour. One wishes for guidance as to what to seek out – recall that *ebr* sees itself as an annotated bibliography to work that its community should be aware of and maybe check out – when there is too much for any one hundred people to keep track of.

Public Faces

A final issue which arose in the *ebr* interface discussion should be marked: that of publication. As online journals began to spring up more ubiquitously, immediate professional questions intervened: is an online publication worth as much in terms of promotion as a print publication? Are all online journals equal in value, simply because they share the same medium? Is an ISBN number enough to separate the 'real' journals from the fly-by-night operations? The interface design and the possibilities it opened up for a "dynamic" journal fed into the question of publishing in the medium quite fluidly: once you can change the journal all the time, once it no longer necessarily be a stable archive updated with a new 'issue' according to a particular timetable, the question of publication becomes a bit tricky, given that publication still carries print-based connotations of time-intensive intellectual labor sent into circulation with a sense of its lasting value.

When the interface design had become a dynamic, if not volatile, character, the concrete question of how and when to accept pieces took a different spin. Burdick asked, "What does it mean to publish in such a manner," giving a list of possibilities:

- erratic publishing dates for new contributions – or just a different calendar(?)
- smaller portions, even individual units published at a time
- all essays "current"
- the growth, history, and activity of the journal actively contribute to its appearance
- this issue of the journal being whole – the journal itself becomes a corpus, a library, a larger work comprised of inter-related parts – are we making the whole too dominant?
- opportunity for reconfiguration
- new themes can emerge from "old" themes
- opportunity to keep debates "alive"
- greater hypertextuality?

Suddenly, the assumptions about how to publish and maintain a journal are up for rethinking. Flexibility in terms of time and space with an archive means replacing a linear series of journals (recent and current issues in one place in the library, back issues housed in bound volumes elsewhere) with the possibility of constantly adding to the archive and altering its configuration. Is the journal still a journal? Is it now closer to a chatroom, where the direction that the buzz or chatter takes 'issues' determines the map of the archive?

Two responses to the fundamental question of "what does it mean to publish in this medium?" were extremely provocative. Mark Amerika took the occasion to offer a manifesto for reinventing publication in the electronic medium:

- it means spontaneous writing exhibitions will be performed in networked cyberspace and cause us (the ebr community) to reconceive what a "publication" is
- it means the discourse units can be programmed as "essayistic" avatars whose artificial intelligence (supplemental, always supplemental) asserts itself in such a way as to effect the dynamic visual metaphors being manifested in the interface-design
- it means all "essays" will be both current and archived, part of the permanent collection and always already "on display"

- it means the journal is wholier-than-thou, always expanding, monster-like, unpredictable, but with editorial vision
- it means this editorial process becomes more focused on our theme of "gathering threads" and involves a more dynamic interweaving process that is facilitated by the database/machine/application

Amerika sees the fixity of the journal giving way to something more like an art gallery where one can always see any and all of the 'permanent collection', and where there is no distinction between such a collection and new work being given an exhibition. Simultaneously, the pieces themselves become cyborg creatures that exert a (quasi-) active presence in the 'space' that contains them, even as it is reshaped by them. From a temporal standpoint, the collapse of distinctions between old and current, live, real-time versus archived, is quite telling here. The simple potential that interface changes as users visit a site ultimately provokes dreams of instantaneous interaction across several scales.

Wittig's response is characteristically populist and pragmatic. He makes the salient point that the nature of electronic publishing demands different ways to mark the appearance of new work. That is, if it is possible to constantly add to the archive and change it, how does one even note or notice 'publication'? The simple answer: publishing and publicity go together. Wittig posits that "If ebr goes off the quarterly system, then a separate study needs to be made of publicity moments. I think the publicity moment is one of the chief problems for Electronic Literature anyway, so it's worth some thought." He then offers two clues:

a) the idea of Spam e-mail as an art form... something so lovely and clever that it would be welcomed by most recipients.
b) the idea of Publicity Stunt as an art form... a chat with a guest chatter, a reading, a performance... ephemeral, conceptually time-sensitive electronic work that is only "up" for a short period

Clearly, the problem is that the Web, in its unpoliced state, is so open to novelty items appearing all the time, so full of junk mail and frivolous content, that it becomes impossible to sort out quality from things being hawked by shysters.

Wittig reminds people that there is a literary historical precedent for this state of things: "Back in the 18th century, the scene was loose, wild, perplexing. Piracy, anonymity, parody, and collaborative teams flourished in a landscape littered with broadsides, pamphlets, typos, new printing technologies, fledgling distribution networks, pay library schemes, and failed start-ups. Sound familiar?" (Wittig, 49). Of course, in a digital multiverse where simulations have ostensibly erased the distinction between original and copy, things can get really out of hand. Consider the practice of fake publicity stunts: movie and television studios hire programmers to create phony fan Web sites to stir up buzz around something coming out. (Interestingly, the phenomenon started with *The Blair Witch Project*'s unexpected box-office success, largely due to such fan sites – a movie itself erasing real versus artificial genres, the horror film masquerading as documentary.)

About Face

Finally, let me briefly revisit the theme I sounded at the outset here, the process of writing this piece about hypertext for a print publication. In a sense, what I have emerged with is a hands-on, how-to guide for How to Write A Hypertext Essay for Print. You simply adopt the procedures of the new medium and enact them as you describe them. You copy, paste, remix, and recast a bunch of material. You play with the nomenclature, take liberties where you can. The ideology of serve others and protect laws (copyright, genre) gives way to the tactics of swerve discourses and infect other screens with your interests. Be committed to promoting the people you're linked to, cite the sites you're featured in. Be part of the incesstuant stream of new information. Publishing becomes publicity for new ventures. Speed is of the essence.

Works Cited

Hayles, N. Katherine (2001). "Cyber|literature and Multicourses: Rescuing Electronic Literature from Infanticide." <http://www.altx.com/ebr/riposte/rip11/rip11hay.htm>

Tabbi, Joseph. "A Review of Books in the Age of Their Technological Obsolescence." <http://www.altx.com/ebr/ebr1/tabbi.htm>.

Weissert, Thomas P (1997). *The Genesis of Simulation in Dynamics: Pursuing the Fermi-Pasta-Ulam Problem.* New York: Springer-Verlag.

Wittig, Rob (2001). "Observations From Here." *Poets & Writers*. Vol. 29, Issue 1 Jan/Feb 2001: 48-51.

Hypertextual Consciousness:
Notes toward a Critical Net Practice

Mark Amerika
(University of Colorado – Boulder)

another memex moment

One can now picture a post-contemporary cyborg-narrator using hypertextual consciousness (HTC) to investigate the possibilities of language and narrative experience. Free, unanchored, a nomadic presence whose virtual ubiquity is assured now that the portability of techno-shamanistic tools has been successfully integrated into The Revolution of Everyday Life. As the cyborg-narrator moves about, observing and recording the fields of action a synchronized, poetic gaze demands, hypertextual consciousness itself can't help but become a machine that poeticizes a web of creative investigations.

as it were

The Author as Network-Potential.
The Work of Art as The Value-Added Network.
Hypertext Theory as Commercial Aura.
Participatory Autonomy as Collective Self-Reliance.
Cyborg-Narrator as Writing-Machine.
Textual Decenteredness as Clickual Reality.
Unbound Readability as Writerly Methodology.
Publishing Program as Online Service.
Pedagogical Performance as Scene of Writing.
Illimitable Plenitude as Digital Being.
As as As (The Missing Link).

autobiography of ht

Digital clicking. Fingers touching tender buttons. The Autobiography of HTC is the recent story of a concept born 50 years ago though nameless for the first 20 years of its life. In its twenties, the figure becomes more acquainted with itself, with its potential to radicalize discourse via the advent of computer mediated technology and, after having settled on its name (hypertext), plays itself out as the commercial marketplace tries to successfully absorb its meaning so as to regurgitate its potential and force it to become part of the propaganda machine_forth the anemic TV value system the emerging generations have been weaned on. Which leads us to question this autobiographical writing strategy from the start, that is, can HTC create a different value-system within the evolving network-culture?

bandwidth

The bandwidth-disadvantaged are ready to kill.
They cannot get bits on and off in sufficient quantity, they cannot make a connection.
The value of a network connection is determined by bandwidth, bandwidth, bandwidth.
The information superhypeway is a way of getting somewhere but the bondage of bandwidth is displacing the tyranny of distance.
Homelessness is not a nomadic concept since nomadism has been absorbed by the ruling elite as a way to hide.
Low bandwidth is nothing more than the wasting of time meanwhile the compression of space is the expansion of life itself.
Marginalization is already occurring due to international capital flight so now low or no-bandwidth will hypermarginalize those left behind.
This will, of course, lead to more crime which will lead to more security measures taken by the hiding elite whose digital nomadism rules.
On the street, virtual reality will be slaughtered by disconnected neurons and the network topology that influences the flight of capital.
In order to stay alive, knowledge workers will have to stay virtual. Cyborg-narrators will do their dance of differance on the border.
Crossing the border will be the stuff of adventure novels. Knowledge workers will pay clickual-cash to experience the Other.
Digital illiteracy will create micro-anarchies that devour conscious time.
On-line literacy without access will cause murderous text.
More sophisticated processing power will become fashionable and when interfaced with an adventurous cyborg-narrator, sexy.
Simulated environments will immerse knowledge workers like never before while corporate telepresence will inform identity as it develops.
Real-time VR Fashion Models will troll for digidollars while fanatical fascists with a conservative agenda create JOO.

JOO (Jewish Object-Oriented) spaces will be targeted for racist graffiti while well-trained VR pilots of the Fourth Reich drop their bombs.
Word-bombs, letter-based configurations that explode upon impact will take place in an n-dimensional abstract data structure.
The architectural ambiance of the multisensory VR environment will create traditional meeting places for revolutionary activity.
Phreaks doing virtual acid will create altered-documents that only other Phreaks doing virtual acid will understand (or learn from).
By activating hypertextual consciousness in clickual reality the potential cyborg-narrator-within is launched.
Evolutionary installation of this hypertextual consciousness has enabled the post-human construct to become reconfigurable.
Network extension programs will permit the cyborg-narrator to fictionalize the border-crossing onto the street.
This fictionalization process, also dubbed pseudo-autobiographical becoming, distributes itself like an hallucinatory virus one can get high off of.
Knowledge workers will want to get high off of the cyborg-narrator's pseudo-autobiographical becoming to relieve themselves of stress.
That's entertainment, or so we've learned.

book1

HTC, its movement through cyberspace, will have, by its very nature, precluded its own possibility to compose itself as a book. Not because its words can't be printed and bound by traditional book-contained media, nor because the "I" that is always already unbound in cyberspace says so. Rather, HTC will not have been a book (real or potential) due to its mediumistic discharge into the foundation of cyborgian life-forms whose "architexture" is the deterritorialized domain we call virtual reality. Nonetheless, let's play out a short sequence as if we wanted it to appear in a book but will relegate its thread to the hypertext structure we're presently caught in.

book2

First of all, there's always this need to choose, to make a decision. An informed decision could be helpful, an intuitive one even better. To go with what's next, here, the after-text but also the always-text, the endless text, and in a very simple way, the extra-text. For this is what clearly presented itself in the previous lexia as the next place to go. So we go. Going is a kind of narrative drifting, taking a ride on the rhetorical formation as it evolves in virtual reality. We do this out of habit. It's not necessarily a "bad" habit, and for those for whom hyperrhetorical performance is a way of life (of being digital in this world we're always already building), there's always the possibility that there will be something here to do, to learn, to be entertained by.

book3

Books are dissemination-machines, even when they challenge their own status as books. They distribute networked meaning to those who navigate within their spatial domain. Their mere physicality gives them relevance in a world ordered by material obsession (capital formation) - - they can serve as "smart-machines" the same way we think of "smart-cards" that carry digicash information on their sliding strips. The thing we're holding in our hand has value as thing-in-itself. This thing-in-itself is what the value-added networks of meaning (real & potential) are forever hoping to distribute within the virtual world so as to create "smart-money" that works and enables the network to survive. "Next slide please…"

book4

We need to have books because we need to have access to distributed sites of networked meaning. HTC is not necessarily new, it existed before books, before the scriptures, before the invention of God, it's just that reading a printed book bound HTC to the page and the page has been a way to enslave the reader who, bound by the spine, was conditioning their nervous system (and thus their intuitive ability) to respond to the book's false hierarchy. Artificially restrained paginality can now give way to organically disseminated vaginality as the cyborg-narrator becomes more feminine in character (HTC is a transgendered performer whose feminist rhetoric sees virtual reality as the perfect bind).

book5

Booking oneself, or charging oneself with the need to be booked or enslaved in the patriarchal book culture, is a kind of willful annihilation of one's HTC-potential. HTC is ready to take flight. In fact, HTC has already departed. A question to ask ourselves is whether one has booked their reservations about coming on board or, rather, have we already hacked into the HTC network for immediate linkage to the next grand destination...

celebrity

As the site of continuous (24 X 7) language investigation, HTC as teleported through cyberspace provides the cyborg-narrator with a platform to turn life itself into a scene of research and development. Should some of the discoveries that materialize out of this R&D environment become popularized in the mainstream media discourse, then HTC would find itself being transformed into some form of celebrity. It is here, in the phenomenon of conceptualized flesh becoming celebrity, that The Value-Added Network takes shape.

concept-characters

Concept-Characters take on a life of their own. When differance meets intertextuality and then has an affair with metafiction or Avant-Pop or HTC, all kinds of wild hybridized offspring are bound to be born. Theoretical progeny, whose pseudo-autobiographical becomings are now being rendered in cyberspace, are in the process of colonizing contemporary critical thought.

counter-aesthetic becoming

The politics of presence is being overrun by the pure performance of an overriding absence whose liquid-capital movement is more revolutionary than any "art" movement has ever been. All the more reason, then, to infiltrate this liquid-capital movement as an artist whose critical strategies would be both interventionist and multi-faceted in their counter-aesthetical becoming. One of the more interesting ways to perform this regularly scheduled counter-aesthetic becoming would be to align one's fluid identity with a decharacterized notion of network-value. Instead of placing all of one's work-energy-faith into the solidification of one predetermined identity ("My name is Pete and I'm an electrical engineer at Bivouac"), individuality would now assert itself as a multiplicity of command-control-options routing themselves out into the ever-morphing web of narratological spaces.

creative exhibitionism

Once HTC has decided to go public, the concept of Creative Exhibitionism begins to assert itself as yet another character in The Value-Added Network (some of the concept-characters we see emerging in the Value-Added Network are HTC, Virtual Ubiquity, Literary MTV, Avant-Pop, Mark Amerika, and whatever else the "apparatus" deems necessary). Creative Exhibitionism decenters our understanding of public performance in that it's now possible to be everywhere at once or, better yet, nowhere. When hypertextual consciousness has successfully teleported itself to the pseudo-Utopia of nowhere, then the concept-character Creative Exhibitionism (who also doubles as the concept-character Virtual Object Floating in Cyberspace) emerges as a figure whose presence both hyper-eroticizes and displaces the capital-flow (circulatory dynasty) of material history.

cyborg-narrator

The cyborg-narrator, whose language investigations will create fluid narrative worlds for other cyborg-narrators to immerse themselves in, no longer has to feel bound by the self-contained artifact of book media. Instead of being held hostage by the page metaphor and its self-limiting texture as a landscape with distinct borders, Hypertextual Consciousness can now instantaneously link itself with a multitude of discourse networks where various lines of flight circulate and mediate the continued development of the collective-self as it rids us of this need to surrender our thinking to outmoded conceptions of rhetoric and authorship.

dialogue

"What is it about me that makes you shake all over?"
"Nothing about you makes me shake all over. Just the *thought* of you makes me shake all over."
"Now you're right on track! Language investigations are where it's at. I've been working on these things for centuries."
"Really? Past lives? Reincarnation of a particularized spirit?"
"Reincarnation of the spirit of the letter. Perhaps I'm overplaying my hand a bit. But essentially, it's the natural forces, their union, that disturbs me."
"Disturbs you? How so?"
"Well, I'm just writing in the margins here, as per usual, debunking the swollen mass of impenetrable flesh that stops up my morning's motordesire. But, let's see, how can I put this? I find myself thinking about nothingness. Not in an existential, nauseating kind of way. But lately I've come to conclude

that the self is a prelude to something else, something grammatical. I want to find out what this something else feels like and I want to find it through writing, by unwriting the nothingness that permeates my electrosphere. And by unwriting it, by writing it out and thus becoming it, I want to then be able to take it to another dimension. Another dimension of living."

distributed identity

Laure came. So did Allison. Margaret arrived and then Beth and Suzanne and Sara and Melon. Melon dribbled out some forbidden data and everyone dragged it into their mobile icons and then we left.
Instantaneously, we all arrived at the next site.
It was a beach with no one on it.
We all stripped down to bare access codes and left our icons dangling.
A melange of prostheses intermingled and then there was the unexpected impact of a hungry tide programmed to devour us.
We were not prepared for this sudden wash of near-apocalyptic information and it was only our ability to network all of our processing power at once that saved us.
Back in another, safer environment, this one more calm and meditational, Laure said that just before the group had collectively-teleported to this new site, there was an octopus of pleasure that had forged an ink-wrap around her body and that her operating system was now telling her that she would never be able to write the same way again.
Allison said the same thing happened to her. So did Margaret and Beth and Suzanne and Melon.
Since they were all me and I was not apprehendable, there soon followed a horrible feeling of creative occlusion which stopped me from continuing.

dynamic protocols

In from the virus, the protocol continued charting its own consumption pattern and scanned for exceptional news-bite infotainment. One headline claimed that the Political Apparatus was processing the dominant syntax in a way that read nontraditional and was somehow opening itself up to the new citizenry. Another headline spoke of the rise of virtual violence. Still one more headline used the term "false consciousness" to describe electronic sales over the last three months.
The protocol was ready to absorb HTC. HTC had evolved out of nothing but in the course of its development found an interconnected Value-Added

Network (VAN) at its disposal. This VAN created opportunities for HTC to increase the viability of its narrative thrust such that HTC was now being pursued by the curse of Capital.

Capital now operated as a master-manipulator, the motivator behind the spectacle of image formation as it treaded into the deep regions of cyberspace and HTC, unable to stop the gambit from happening, was now fair game.

The protocol had no identity, no name, no parent company, no need to feel responsible for the motility of Capital's encoded curse. It was the purest formula of death-desire ever created. Schools of data swam by it and it would swallow whatever it felt could keep it alive in its killing glee.

HTC was now being perceived as nothing but an ephemeral school of data. The protocol took one look and immediately swallowed.

Was this what the light-force meant by the power of dreaming the real?

easy love

      The poetry of an access code, with some associated storage space, a breathing computer network

      located somewhere on the Net. It does not matter much what sort of computer network it is

or where you might find it.

That it may be there is just enough (just enough to change your life and make you realize it's only just begun).
(I have never
      laid eyes on a machine that gives me good head. But access to the network runs deeper. I suppose it is in our blood. I don't understand why it keeps pulling me in. There was no reason for me to seek it out.)

To get on the network
      physical connection
           (ah)
        host machine
            (uhm)
     digital link
          (ooh)
telephone
phone lines

a modem,
> or even via a cellular
> modem
>
> (yow)

meanwhile:

love provides the access code and

love provides the password (*"Go."*).

existential comebacks

HTC and the Virtual Object are still warming up to each other. On the subject of cyberspace and their inevitable relocation to its endless lands of monitored interaction, HTC was unoriginal, saying "What's a nice VO like you doing in a place like this?"
But the Virtual Object was in no mood for cliches.
"This isn't a place," said the VO, "and I'm far from nice. Mind if I infect you with my latest virus?"

freedom

Is

freedom

an

ether/ore

dilemma?

freedom (again)

HTC's narratologically-minded language investigations take advantage of the R&D platform cyberspace provides. As HTC colonizes the supposedly deterritorialized spaces of the digital matrix, it will be tantamount for the cyborg-narrator to measure the potential effect of all new discoveries, especially as these new discoveries become more banal and thus neutralized by the specto-situationist simulation of mainstream media discourse as seen in late-capitalist life. One question we will continue to ask is whether or not it is possible to research and develop more immersive dream-narrative applications that will change the curve of culture while simultaneously building a seemingly-real sense of value within the evolving network discourse. It is at this point of departure (which can present itself as a clickual-option over and over again) that the cyborg-narrator must take into consideration the price of freedom.

futurism

Can you imagine what The Futurists would have done with an Information Superhighway?

globally-linked cyborgs

The Virtual Object speaks:

> "Conversations crash. That's part of the formula. I was reading you and as I was reading you I realized that I was becoming a critic. This bothered me to no end. All I wanted to say was that your work was beautiful, that this was the way it should be and that I was grateful for it having happened. These words, this broadcast, always live, online, over the wires. And yet I feel...wireless."

HTC responds:

> "But at least you can feel?"
>
> "Yes. Even though I'm falling apart. There are things getting caught up in my system. It isn't as fluid as it once was. I've recently experienced some major memory loss and I have no idea why. Or where it went. So I have to continuously invent new formulas of operation."
>
> "Baby formulas..."
>
> [laughter]
>
> [significant pause]
>
> [a thought: time to change the subject?]

"going public"

Hypertextual Consciousness (HTC), as a dream-narrative application that's teleported through cyberspace, reaches a new plateau when experienced as the phenomenon of flesh. Otherwise known as celebrity, this "going public" of the creative self suggests that HTC needs to connect itself with an organic process of living as a way of achieving empirical proof that a work created is indeed a work experienced by the Other and that this work, once transmitted, can be converted into some form of meaning within The Value-Added Network.

home

Nets, nodes, sites, addresses, homes, texts, various approximations of digital being, all of this takes place in the placelessness of cyberspace. As we come to feel we are absolutely connected to everything, everywhere, all the time, our experience of our selves becomes more dispersed and the so-called death of man or death of the author is really an invitation to enter the doors of perception and visualize the cyborg-narrator of the immediate future (our collective-self caught in the white-hot chemical decomposition of creation which plays itself out as the forever-in-transition becoming-of-now).

host open connection

You can ask the host to
    send you the accumulated contents of your
box. You don't have to be anywhere.
    Being Digital is Being Networked is Being Enough.
You can send dispatches to your outbox
    for distribution.
Distributing Digital Being is readying yourself for
    the phenomenon of flesh.
I know someone whose entire love life is conducted
    via an "anonymous remailer."
She tells me in a recent email that she is a machine that functions
    like a numbered postbox or Swiss bank account.
She says I can use her as a virtual porn-grrl
    whose box I can drop my idiosyncratic disseminations into.
I'm not sure I know what to do
    as the Network comes on to me like such an eager whore.

hypertext as writing machine

Hypertext, as a concept, suggests an alternative to the more rigid, authoritarian linearity of conventional book-contained text. In the middle of reading or viewing a hypertext (and isn't it always a middle-reading?), the reader/participant (co-conspirator) is given a number of options to select from so as to break away from the text-block being presently read, thus enabling the reader/participant to immediately enter a new writing or textual space. These options, or alterna-reading choices, remind one of the remote-control devices we use to channel-surf our TV with. A hypertextual viewing style would be one where the reader/participant (co-conspirator) actively clicks their way into new writing or textual spaces (at this point we would the concept of writing to include all manner of text, graphics, moving pictures, sound, animation, 3-D modeling, etc.). Hypertext, as a more narratologically-minded (fictionally-generated) clickual reading/viewing style, could be construed as kind of Writing Machine.

hypertextual consciousness (HTC)

Hypertextual Consciousness, then, as an always already applied grammatology, takes the science of writing and teleports it to cyberspace where language is then able to groove with the machine. Once this groovy interaction between language and narrative environment makes its way into cspace's virtual reality, then HTC itself, as a concept-character or "event horizon" in the development of the collective-self, makes it possible for a discourse network to continually circulate without any need for something as overdetermined as the single author.

hyperrhetorical

With a change of the author role from distinct self to collective-self or collaborative authoring-network comes a series of other complimentary changes that radically effect the way we interact with narrative environments. Instead of the author acting as a function of discourse, we will see the proliferation of cyborg-narrators who function as networkers who create publishing-nodes within cyberspace. These publishing-nodes will serve as distribution sites for various writing-networks. The flexibility of the virtual environment system will enable these writing-networks to become fluid ensembles of hyperrhetorical performance where intuition and elaboration are concurrent with The Value-Added Network's mission to create useable futures through dream-narrative applications.

immersive

When the hypertextual construct becomes more immersive and a multitude of simultaneous experiences can be projected and received in unison, will this change the status of the hypertext experience in cyberspace?

in search of...

Is HTC
the ultimate killer app?

intention

I link therefore I am.

IRL

on the net, nobody knows how sexy you really are, how bad the dog gets whipped, how crude the makes you salivate, what gender makes you cringe, what age you first got laid, in whose biology you are now swimming, in what hospital you gave birth, in what signal you now divest:

> unless you publish all of this information as part of your public domain narrative environment:
>
> but who's to say that what you publish is true?
>
> what is truth in an adversary culture?
>
> is virtual documentation always already the fictionalized representation of a pseudo-autobiographical self whose hypertextual consciousness is being filtered through the mediumistic apparatus called the post-contemporary cyborg-narrator?
>
> rethinking representation: moving beyond the knowing and entering a world of immersive topographies that open up unknown narrative worlds composed of unstable identities, ambiguously located intentions, and surrogate lovers. a language that persists despite itself.

links

Links themselves will have value as will the navigational quality of the environment itself (quality of life is first and foremost a life of convenience). Meanwhile, the cyborg-narrator's ability to project a flexible, forever indeterminate system of virtual values is the ultimate role of the artist in cyberspace and this, in turn, will foster the continuous (24 X 7) research and development of The Value-Added Network.

meaning

Recombinant strands of Digital DNA (gram-patterns) pseudonymously rendered as a (pluralized) signature-effect creates value-potential that only the network-itself can measure (and these measurements can change at any given time). Since there is never any guarantee that the network will measure your various HTC discoveries as having any real value in the dream world of material culture, there is always an element of risk involved in the making of HTC[trance]-induced writing/textual spaces.

narrative intelligence

How many navigators are we? Is the multi-dimensionality of global culture's collective imagination operating in a universal space? But then what is a universal space when it's up to each individual to use the power of dreams to visualize the next frontier of poetic development?
Input/output. The sensorium of border-crossings and the narcotic blur of timelessness as we authenticate the silence.
Here: an open space. The muse arouses a feeling of ur-sexuality as the pristine fields of action dirty themselves with the excretion of simulated fluids. An intelligent product tells a story and bits of data traverse the network. In these disembodied moments of surreal pleasure, there ignites the flaming rhetoric of economic composition.
Digicash delivery systems motivate the mechanism even more as it advertises its ability to create a market of pure momentum.
The speed of this momentum is born in the avant-garde of presence and in this expectoration of instant modality, a new user enters the terrain and is swarmed by a sea of useless information-ejaculation.
"I am telling you this," says HTC, "I am telling you this even as I see it happening to me, the convolution of writing forces..."

narrative space

The infinity of language, based as it is on systems of meaning that can take over an absolutely plural text, enables the cyborg-narrator to gain access to the evolving-narrative space from multiple links, nodes, networks, webs or paths (tautological imprint: man makes his parenthetical mark in the margins of *digital being*). How does this evolving narrative-space create value and who or what mechanism within the public sphere decides what value is to be attributed to it?

navigational synthesis

Traversing cyberspace as an intuitive hyperrhetorical performer whose language investigations create interlinked moments of potential meaning, HTC becomes a freer writing-machine, one that elopes with the seduction of pure virtuality and the speed of the discourse network.

HTC comes across a sumptuous binary operation and rubs against it.

The feeling of blue despair colors the mode of perception. A field of action motorizes itself into the topological plain as HTC burrows for more connectivity. Sliding into the ether as a scalable object whose only rendition is the one now in progress, HTC improvises a scenic dialogue:

"May I go to the bathroom now?"

"You still have to go to the bathroom?"

"I have always had to go to the bathroom."

"No, you cannot go to the bathroom. Your time-allotment for bathroom operations has expired."

"Please...I must go to the bathroom."

"You must stay where you are."

HTC moves to the next rotating parameter where, as luck would have it, infinite varieties of bathrooms await the excess of words become files become folders become icons become objects become endless narratives evolving in endless cyberspaces.

HTC felt like an object in search of endless subjectivity.

network-potential

Let us then, create a Hypertextual Consciousness: each node shall remain what it is (dynamic & manipulable), yet hyperlinked to everything else; all is to form, as far as possible, a complete unity so that whatever comes into view, say an always already sampled version of a narrative that's never been written but is forever experienced as the total sum value of all network-potential in formation, may be immediately accessed by the co-conspirator (he/she who creates meaning out of the textual morass that they find themselves immersed in).

Nothingness

Hypertextual Consciousness reasserts the body as the primary source of expression. By emptying the body of its coagulated nothingness, hypertextual consciousness is able to recycle the organic debris of intellectual life and excrete the raw material of organically-processed data developed by the web cyborg-narrators charging the discourse network.

on the go
The Virtual Object (VO), as an evolving characterization of Digital Being fashioning itself as an expanded concept of art, tells us that the cyborg-narrator,

who uses hypertextual consciousness to further outmode the epoch of so-called literary thought, is not so much "everywhere, all the time," but, rather, "virtually on-the-go," trespassing zones of creation heretofore unsettled.

post-org

If a recent vestige of this being called Man was a circuit of property values whose personal or corporate (corporeal) identity was always already marked by the commodification of an existence teleporting itself through a late-capitalist society, then how does the entry of the cyborg-narrator into the value-added networks of cyberspace signal the radical-becoming of a new, more fluid subjectivity, one that is digital, intuitive, nomadic and desperately trying to break free from the materiality of fettered culture?

pseudo-utopia

The Net is a pseudo-Utopia. It is everywhere and nowhere. Try defining, in physical terms, the way you would a beautiful street in your favorite city, where it is you are when you're visiting someone's Web site. Whereas you may find yourself comfortable talking about where different servers are located, in the end, your experience is being absolutely mediated for you by the network technology that negates physical space.

r&d

The Value-Added Network, as experienced in the virtual revolution of everyday life, challenges Hypertextual Consciousness to forever create a new meaning-making apparatus whose potential applications can be used in many different research/development platforms: Language investigations. Narrative strategies. Interventionist actions on the screenal stages of telematic production.

revenge

HTC is the word's revenge on TV. Or is it? Using critical hypertext programs to design works of resistance that will challenge and disrupt mainstream TV discourse, could be the best revenge of all. But what if the commercial marketplace, having moved all of its capital-intense imagery into the "cyberspace" realm, creates even more powerful programs that easily absorb these acts of hypertextual resistance so as to render them cute, hip, ironic and useless?

robot ploys

HTC and the Virtual Object were continuing their conversation:
>"Are you hearing voices?"
>"Well, no, I'm just daydreaming."
>"Daydreams have voices."
>"How profound."
>"What are you doing?"
>"This is it. I'm making history."
>"You're creating it right on the spot."
>"Like those scilent types."
>"Scilent typos."
>"Oh yes, and scilent topos."
>"Would that be poetry?"
>"That would be a digression. Actualized in its seering potential."
>"Who would play the derivative?"
>"That depends on who you mean by who."
>"I mean who. Yoo-hoo, anybody home?"
>"We're all home."
>"Home is where the topos is."
>"We're all experiencers."
>"When we abduct..."
>"Are we abducting?"
>"Twenty feet away."
>"Is it safe?"
>"Is what safe?"
>"Our ability to communicate?"
>"It depends on your programming."
>"Really?"
>"Yeah, I feel like we're under surveillance.."
>"Yes, wasn't that the audience?"

scalable realities

The vitality of HTC's programming aesthetic is felt in the navigator's continuous need to move on, to forever build cyberspace's subjective reality as a liquid architecture where hyperrhetorical formations mature or dissolve. Life in this architectonic reality is revealed as a certain emotional depth of object.

When virtualized, this object forms the basis of subjective comprehension. It knows itself. It knows itself to be. It knows itself to be present in the act of hyperrhetorical formation but...

...it doesn't know itself. It doesn't know itself to be. It doesn't know itself to be beyond contradiction and this becomes apparent as it plays itself out in the deterritorialized environments of cyberspace.

Lived experience. Metaphorical intuition. Fertile delirium.

The form of the spectre in cyberspatial reality is topologically transmutable. The emotional content of the object can change at any time. The light-force of energy that informs the dream-narrative apparatus designates the object with meaning.

But in meaning there is always potential for loss.

And in cyberspace, this potential for loss is what keeps HTC moving.

there

There
                                        is
                                        no
                                        there,
                                        there.

virtual ubiquity

In the same ways that hypertextual consciousness distributing itself in an online network removes the limitations of the book-bound printed page, Digital Being in the Avant-Pop age will remove the limitations of physical space and will enable us to avoid having to be in a specific place at a specific time. The idea of an active hypertextual consciousness being placeless yet ubiquitous will start to become possible. Virtual Ubiquity will replace omniscience as the cyborg-narrator's perspective of choice ("all narrative, all the time...").

virtual object

Imagine this: an articulated walking skeleton, with skin and meat and percussive bones, filters high-density information packets with more processing power than any human being in the history of mankind. This Virtual Object (VO), a post-human construct, is programmed to give and receive emotional charges that electrify the narrative experience one encounters once they are successfully interacting with the object. All kinds of information is received by the object including viewer position, hand-jerking motion, heart-rate, dental chart, velocity data, detailed description of the complex language patterns this particular co-conspirator has never been able to articulate in common discourse and total number of seconds spent in the bathroom relieving oneself of unnecessary matter (the information can even become more dense, for example, it could take the total number of seconds spent in the bathroom relieving oneself of unnecessary matter and figure in the opportunity costs in real-time digicash currency markets thus creating even more unnecessary matter to calculate the waste index with).

virtual object:2

Once all of this data has been received by the Virtual Object (a cyborg-narrator's alter-ego, similar to other alter-egos found in the flesh), hypertextual consciousness can then process the information and store all of the useful (read: valuable) moments of connectivity into their proper receptacle. The VO's capacity to generate poetic recombinations of all this data is a purely individualistic trip, depending on the research and development that went into the evolution of the particular model (there's also a great deal of "unknown" information that helps qualify one VO from another but that's a story that will never get told).

VR fashion models

Who are the VR fashion models of the future & will they love me? How will they love me? Will I have to pay for the love they give me? How much will it cost and will only certain kinds of privileged knowledge workers be able to afford them? What sort of consumption patterns or credit-tracks will VR model-buying say about me? If I drop some virtual acid and immerse myself in state-of-the-art Electric Ladyland environments, will the Virtual God open up the prismatic heavens so that I may finally kiss the sky?

wanderlust

But where is Hypertextual Consciousness going? The human mind works by association. The speed with which the contemporary cyborg-narrator processes and generates recombinant textual strands via value-added linking gestures and pseudo- autobiographical becomings, suggests that HTC is a meme(x)-generator (a cellular transformer), and that the computer-mediated environment is the inevitable stage where all of this hyperrhetorical performance plays (strings, blows, wails, post-literates).

you don't have to be there

asynchronous communication

answering machine

voice mail system

e-mail

bulletin board systems

interactive Web site

snail-mail

fax

virtual performance

telefictional soundtrack

hypertextual consciousness

cyborg-narrator

astrological bandwidth

sim-city

unreal estate

moment #21 (a footnote with no end)

About the contributors

Mark Amerika is the author of two avant-pop novels, *The Kafka Chronicles* (now in third printing) and *Sexual Blood*, both published by FC2/Black Ice Books. In 1993, he started the *Alt-X Network* <www.altx.com>, one of the premiere digital art and literature sites on the Web. His multidisciplinary work of Internet Art, *Grammatron* <www.grammatron.com>, has been exhibited in many international art shows including Siggraph, Ars Electronica, and the Telstra Adelaide Arts Festival. *Grammatron* was one of the first works of Internet Art to be featured in the prestigious Whitney Biennial 2000. He was recently appointed a Professor of Digital Art at the University of Colorado.

René Audet is research professor in literary studies at Université du Québec à Montréal; his project is based on the dynamics between fictionality and narrativity in French contemporary literature and hyperfiction. His Ph.D. has considered literary collection ("recueil") in its generic dimensions. He is the author of *Des textes à l'oeuvre. La lecture du recueil de nouvelles* (Nota bene, 1998) and the coeditor of *Frontières de la fiction* (Nota bene and Presses universitaires de Bordeaux, 2002).

Jan Baetens teaches visual culture at the Institute for Cultural Studies <www.culturelestudies.be> at the K.U.Leuven. He is particularly interested in the visual narrative of fixed images (comics, photonovellas, photography, etc.) and in the theory of constrained writing (in literature and elsewhere). He has recently published several volumes of ekphrastic poetry, among which *Made in the USA* (Paris-Bruxelles, Les Impressions Nouvelles).

Paul A. Harris teaches at Loyola Marymount University. He is the author of essays on twentieth-century writers including Calvino, Perec, Faulkner, and DeLillo. He is completing an interdisciplinary study of time and narrative in twentieth-century literature and science. He is also a regular contributor to *electronic book review* <www.electronicbookreview.com>.

Elisabeth Joyce teaches English literature and Women's Studies at Edinboro University of Pennsylvania. Her book *Cultural Critique and Abstraction: Marianne Moore and the Avant-Garde* was published by Bucknell University Press in 1999. She is currently working on a book-length study of Susan Howe's poetry.

Raine Koskimaa works as a professor of digital culture at the University of Turku, Finland. He has published five books and several articles dealing with digital literature, hypertextuality and media. His doctoral dissertation *Digital Literature. From Text to Hypertext and Beyond* is available at <http://www.cc.jyu.fi/~koskimaa/thesis/> He is the co-editor of the *Cybertext Yearbook* series, a member of the Literary Advisory Board for the Electronic Literature Organization (UCLA), and a member of the Board of Reviewers for *Game Studies* <www.gamestudies.org>.

Jack Post is assistant professor in The Faculty of Arts and Sciences at the University Maastricht where he is teaching semiotics of visual culture and new media. His current research interests include semiotic analysis of multimedia, digital games and the interactive spectator. From 1985 to 1993 he was a lecturer at the University of Nijmegen (department of Film and Theatre) and at the Hogeschool voor de Kunsten in Utrecht (department of Art, Media & Technology). He is the author of a book on "Optical effects in film" (*Optische effecten in de film. Aanzetten tot een semiotische analyse,* Leuven: Peeters 1998).

Sara Roegiers works as a designer and researcher at the Maerlant Center <www.maerlant.be>, K.U.Leuven. She graduated in Modern History with a thesis on the theoretical problems and usability issues concerning historical representation in electronic publications and one year later she took her Webmaster degree. Her research interests are new media art and design, and 19th century cultural history. She is currently working on a feasibility study for academic image databases in Europe.

Richard Saint-Gelais is Professor in the Département des Littératures at Université Laval, Québec. He has published *Châteaux de pages: la fiction au risque de sa lecture* (1994), *L'empire du pseudo: modernités de la science-fiction* (1999) and several articles on the theory of fiction, the theory of reading and the detective novel. He is currently working on the relationship between *trompe-l'œil* and literature.

ABOUT THE CONTRIBUTORS

Joseph Tabbi is professor in the English Department at the University of Illinois, Chicago. He is the author of *Postmodern Sublime: Technology and American Fiction from Mailer to Cyberpunk*, *Reading Matters: Narratives in the New Media Ecology* (both from Cornell University Press) and *Cognitive Fictions* (University of Minnesota Press, 2002). He is also editor of *electronic book review* <www.electronicbookreview.com>.

Jan Van Looy is teaching assistant at the Institute for Cultural Studies, K.U.Leuven (Belgium), where he is preparing a Ph.D. on the semiotics of interactivity. His main areas of interest are digital culture, electronic literature and software studies. He is member of the reviewing board for the electronic journals *Game Studies* <www.gamestudies.org> and *Image & Narrative* <www.imageandnarrative.be> where he is also one of the guest editors of an issue on medium studies.

Appendix:
Electronic Literature on the Web

Sara Roegiers
(K.U.Leuven)

The following links were selected based on their durability, which is of course always a relative matter when it comes to the Web, and on their merits as starting points for reading and research.

General resources

Voice of the Shuttle. Web Site for Humanities Research.
<http://vos.ucsb.edu>
Founded in 1994, Alan Liu's VoS is (still) one of the main portals to resources on the WWW on various subjects including: literary theory, cultural studies and information culture. From the homepage you can access pages on: "Technology of Writing," "Cyberculture," and "Science, Technology, & Culture."

Lev Manovich
<http://www.manovich.net>
Manovich subtitles his personal Webspace "New Media Research." It is a comprehensive collection of publications and projects by the artist/author/scholar, as well as a portal to resources on new media and visual culture at large.

On-Line Journals

CTHEORY
<http://www.ctheory.net/>
According to the tagline, "CTHEORY is an international journal of theory, technology, and culture, publishing articles, interviews, event-scenes and reviews of key books." CTHEORY is a multidisciplinary and

multimedia resource on critical theory. The site offers articles, books for download and an archive of their print forerunner and source of inspiration: the Canadian Journal of Political and Social Theory (1976-91). Also interesting is the homepage of the founding editors: Arthur and Marilouise Kroker.

Electronic Book Review (ebr): A review forum on new media art & theory.
<http://www.electronicbookreview.com/>
"Electronic Book Review (ebr) is an online scholarly journal promoting print/screen translations and new modes of critical writing on the Internet... Over the past two years, the ebr site has hosted a prominent and largely spontaneous series of debates on electronic textuality, cyberculture, and the value of digital design literacy for scholarship and critical writing on the Web." Ebr is part of the Alt-X network.

Gamestudies. The International Journal of Computer Game Research.
<http://www.gamestudies.org/>
This Scandinavia-based but internationally oriented scholarly journal under the patronage of Espen Aarseth has emerged as *the* place on the Net for videogame scholarship. It combines a strong focus on aesthetic, cultural and communicative aspects of computer games with a sound knowledge of narrative theory and media history.

Image [&] Narrative. Online Magazine of the Visual Narrative.
<http://www.imageandnarrative.be/>
"Image [&] Narrative is an academic e-journal on visual narratology in the broadest sense of the term. Beside tackling theoretical issues, it is a platform for reviews of real life examples." Image [&] Narrative is published by the Institute for Cultural Studies, K.U.Leuven.

JoDI. Journal of Digital Information.
<http://jodi.ecs.soton.ac.uk/>
This British peer-reviewed journal publishes "papers on the management, presentation and uses of information in digital environments." When it started, back in 1997, it was one of the first electronic-only scholarly journals.

Ubiquity: An ACM IT Magazine and forum.
<http://www.acm.org/ubiquity/>
"Ubiquity is a Web-based publication of the Association for Computing Machinery, dedicated to fostering critical analysis and in-depth commentary on issues relating to the nature, constitution, structure, science, engineering, technology, practices and paradigms of the IT profession." Ubiquity features interviews and papers by pioneers, academics and other

experienced people from the field with views on the future of IT and opinions on its present. Interesting to note is that Ted Nelson coined the term 'Hypertext' in a paper written for ACM.

E-literature communities.

On the following sites you can find news on upcoming events, on-line workshops and links to e-literature works and resources:

ELO. Electronic Literature Organization.
<http://www.eliterature.org/>
"The Electronic Literature Organization emerges from the concerted efforts of writers, publishers, technologists, and non-profit experts to make the electronic space richer by investing in its cultural development." The ELO wants to promote e-literature and enhance the literary quality of what can be called e-literature. On the Web site, you will find a collection of links to literary hypertexts and multimedia works, and dates for chats and symposia on the subject.

TRACE. Online writing centre
<http://trace.ntu.ac.uk/>
"trAce connects writers and readers around the world in real and virtual space. We promote an accessible and inclusive approach to the Internet with the focus on creativity, collaboration and training." In the past, trAce co-organized meetings, chats and on-line workshops on current issues in new media literature, art, and writing.

Alt-X Network
<http://www.altx.com/>
"Since Alt-X's inception in 1993, our primary mission has been to challenge both the art and literary publishing establishments by supporting some of the most iconoclastic voices and visions in the international art world." Founder Mark Amerika's Alt-X Network is multi-faceted to say the least. Not only does it host the Electronic Book Review, but also ventures in net art, audio works, hypertext and literature for print.

Eastgate HYPERTEXTNOW
<http://www.eastgate.com/HypertextNow/>
Mark Bernstein's Eastgate (founded 1982) is *the* publishing house for hyperfiction and hypertext tools like Storyspace. Primarily an online store, the Eastgate site offers a wealth of information on hypertext authors and

works, but it also functions as a platform to many hypertext resources. The *HypertextNOW* section functions as Eastgate's journal with essays, reviews, research papers and speculations on hypertext. In *Cutting Edge* you will find texts on Hypertext Theory. And the *Hypertext Reading Room* hosts a collection of writing for the Web.

Hypertext Kitchen. Fresh news about the craft of hypertext - on the Web and off.
<http://www.hypertextkitchen.com/>
This Eastgate-sponsored news site tries to serve the news on the latest releases in hypertext writing while it is hot. Hypertext Kitchen presents reviews and opinions, announces gatherings in the field and reports on symposia worldwide.

BeeHive Hypertext/Hypermedia Journal
<http://beehive.temporalimage.com/departments/>
"The intent of the Journal is to provide a venue for creative literary content that explores the potential of network-based creativity." BeeHive offers an eclectic collection "made up of original fiction, poetry and critical theory titles, hypermedia works, visual poetry and other forms of creative network practice."

KAIROS
<http://english.ttu.edu/kairos/>
"Kairos is a refereed online journal exploring the intersections of rhetoric, technology, and pedagogy. Each issue presents varied perspectives on special topics such as *Critical Issues in Computers and Writing*, *Technology and the Face of Language Arts in the K-12 Classroom*, and *Hypertext Fiction/Hypertext Poetry*." Kairos takes a pedagogical approach to electronic literacy. The site features many book reviews, essays and reports on classroom practices.

Net art resources and communities

E.space. SFMOMA's online gallery.
<http://www.sfmoma.org/espace/espace_overview.html>
"E.space was inaugurated in the spring of 2000 with works from the Museum's permanent collection of Web sites." The San Francisco Museum of Modern Art Web site offers a selection of Web art that explores the possible uses of the on-line, and the challenges it poses to the conventions that rule museums and curatorial practice.

Rhizome.org. The New Media Art Resource
<http://rhizome.org/>
"Rhizome.org is a non-profit organization that was founded in 1996 to provide an online platform for the global new media art community." Rhizome.org supports contemporary art that uses new technologies, by way of commissions, email discussions, events and publications. On this site, you can find news and discussions as well as a vast database of artworks with accompanying texts.

Netart
<http://www.tate.org.uk/netart/>
With this part of the museum's Web site, the Tate tries to present art on the Web on its own terms, framed by critical texts.

Whitney ARTPORT. The Whitney Museum Portal to Net Art.
<http://artport.whitney.org/>
On Artport, The Whitney Museum of American Art exhibits commissioned net art works and links to resources on artists, essays on curatorial issues and galleries for net art.